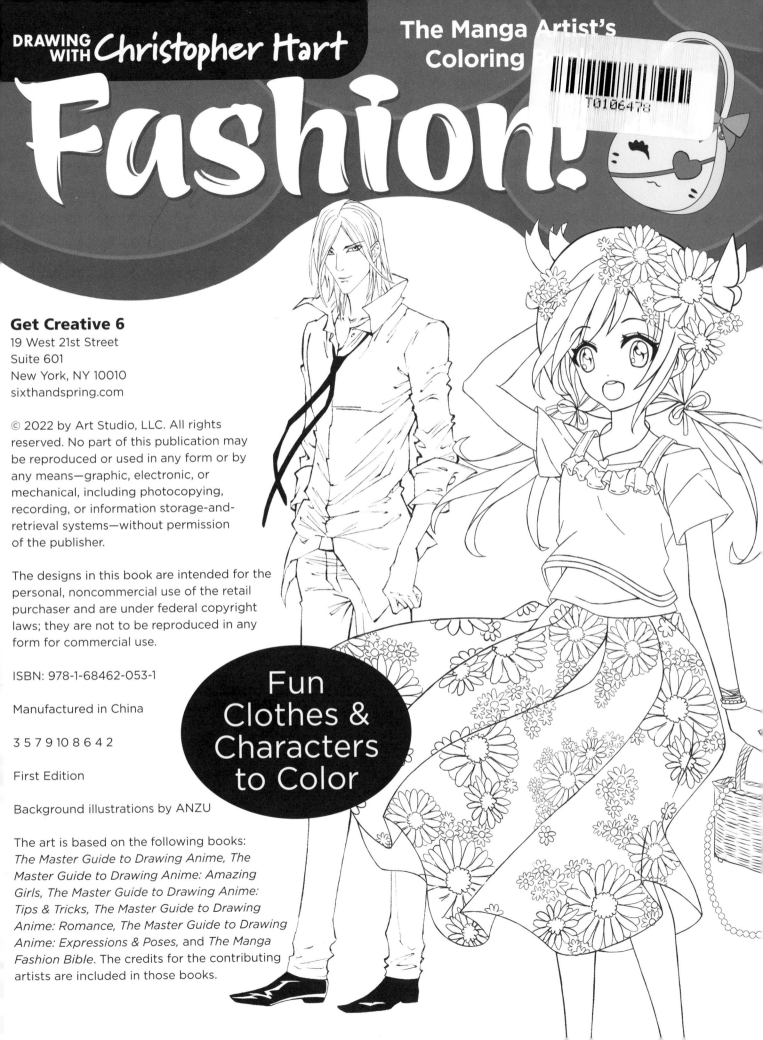

DRAWING WITH Christopher Hart

The Manga Artist's Coloring

Fashion!

Fun Clothes & Characters to Color

Get Creative 6
19 West 21st Street
Suite 601
New York, NY 10010
sixthandspring.com

ISBN: 978-1-68462-053-1

Manufactured in China

3 5 7 9 10 8 6 4 2

First Edition

Background illustrations by ANZU

The art is based on the following books: *The Master Guide to Drawing Anime, The Master Guide to Drawing Anime: Amazing Girls, The Master Guide to Drawing Anime: Tips & Tricks, The Master Guide to Drawing Anime: Romance, The Master Guide to Drawing Anime: Expressions & Poses,* and *The Manga Fashion Bible.* The credits for the contributing artists are included in those books.

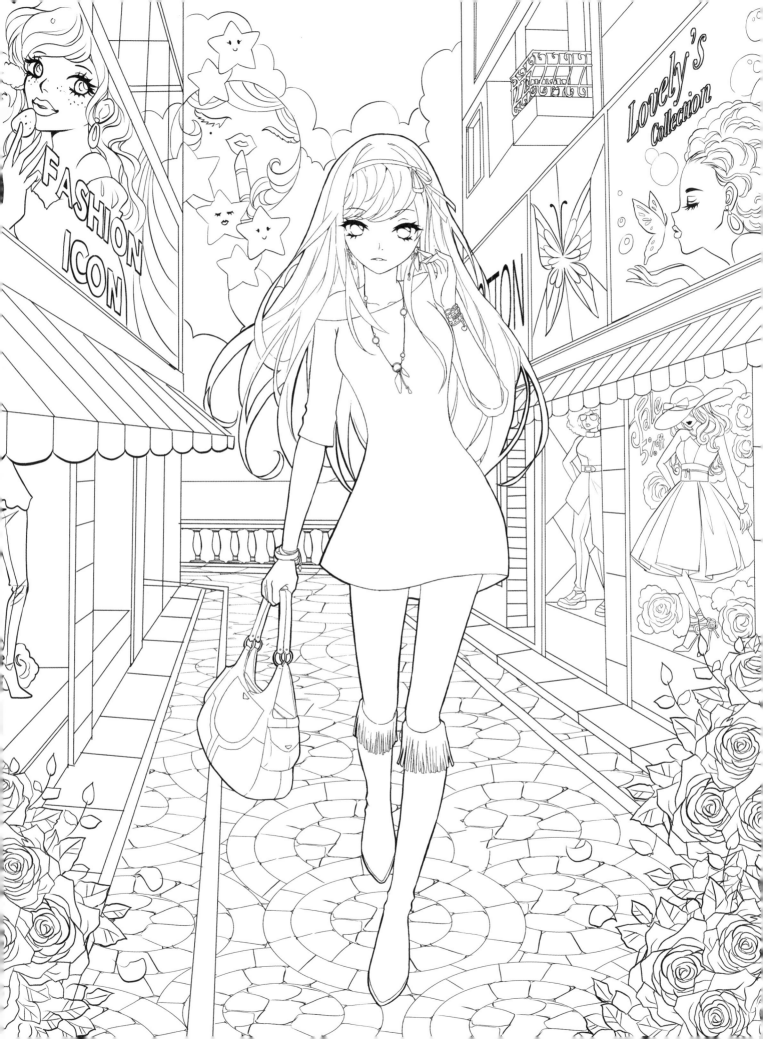

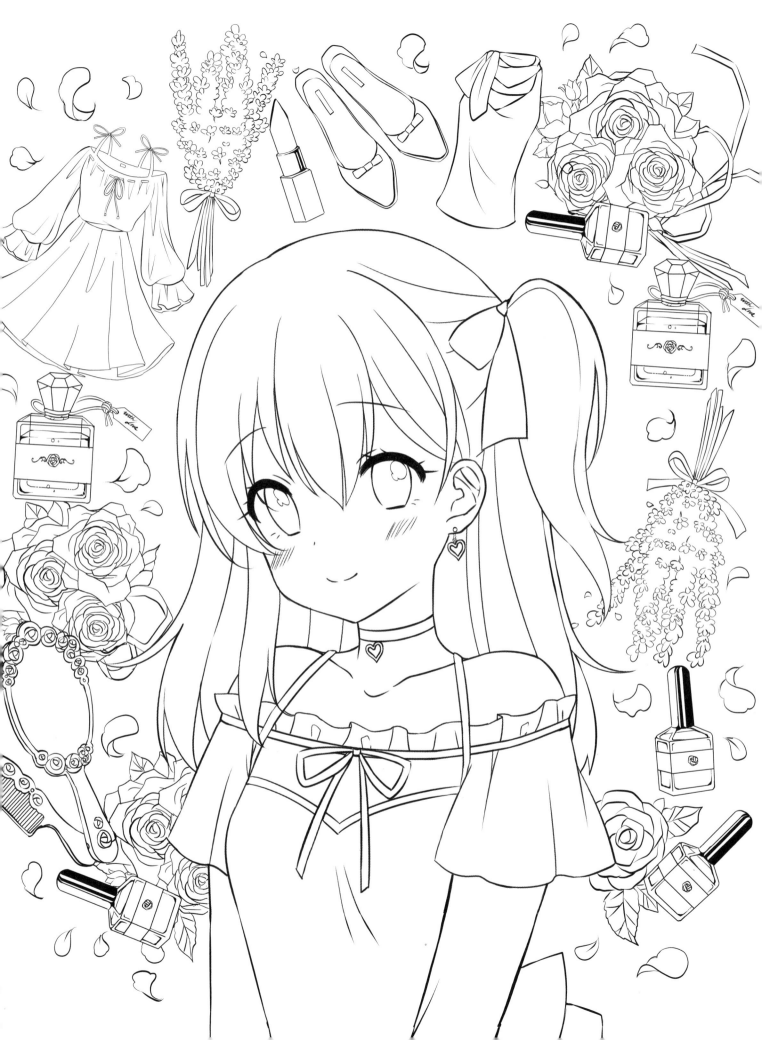

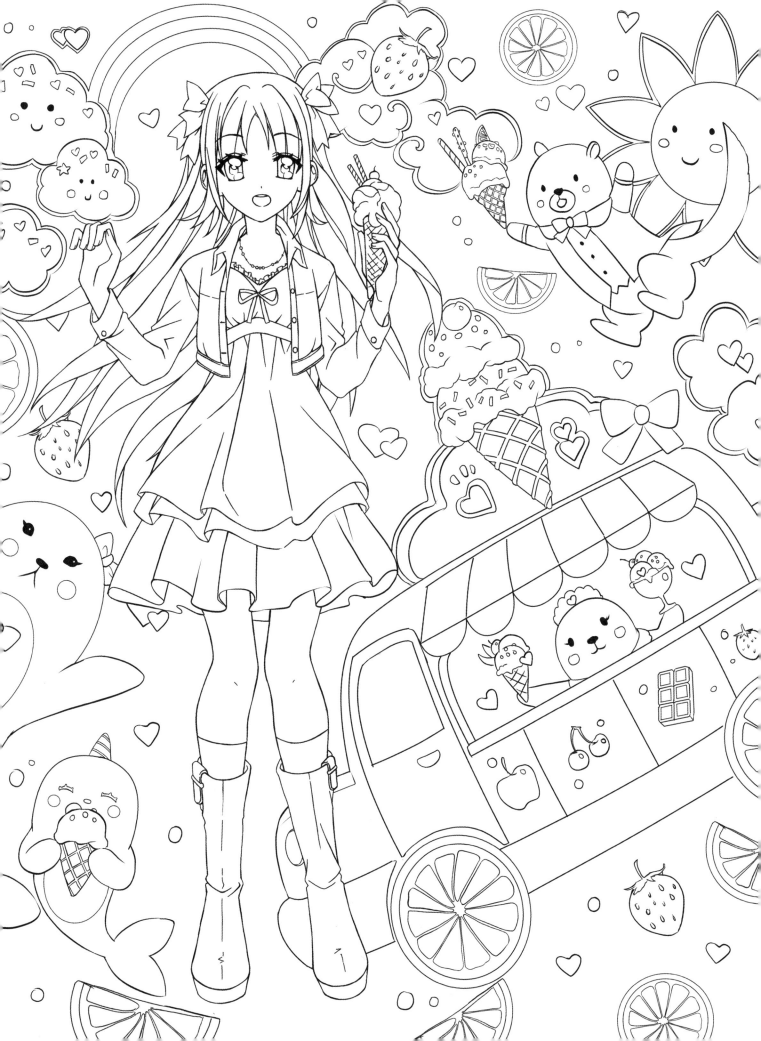

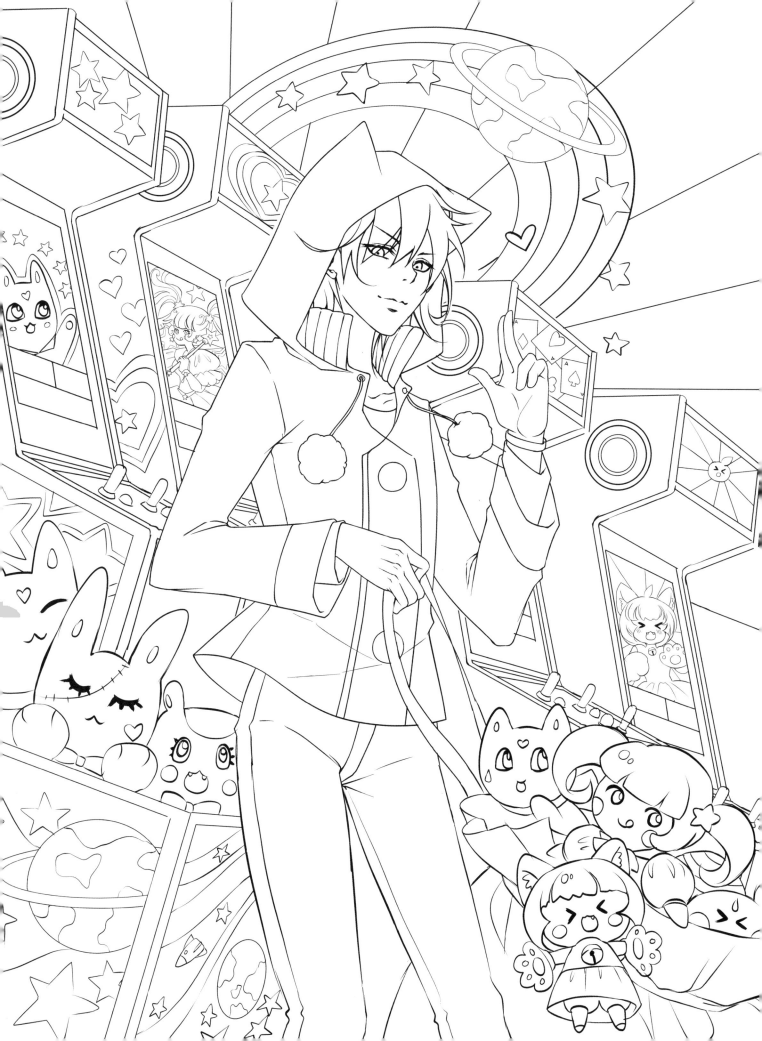

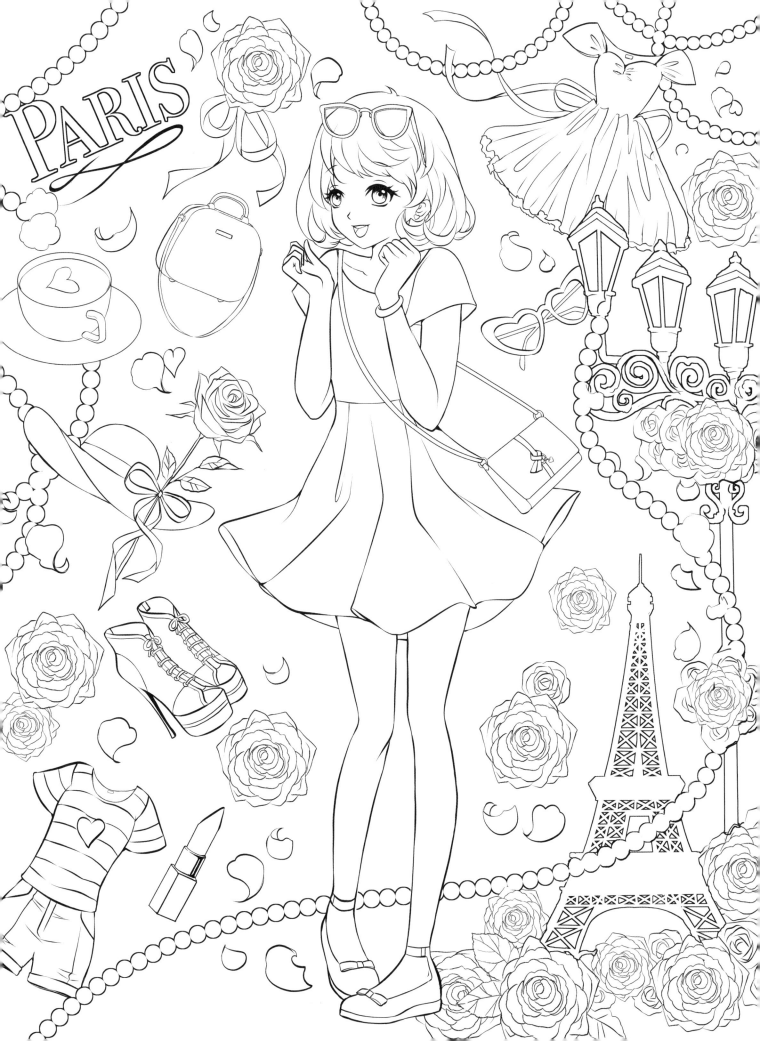

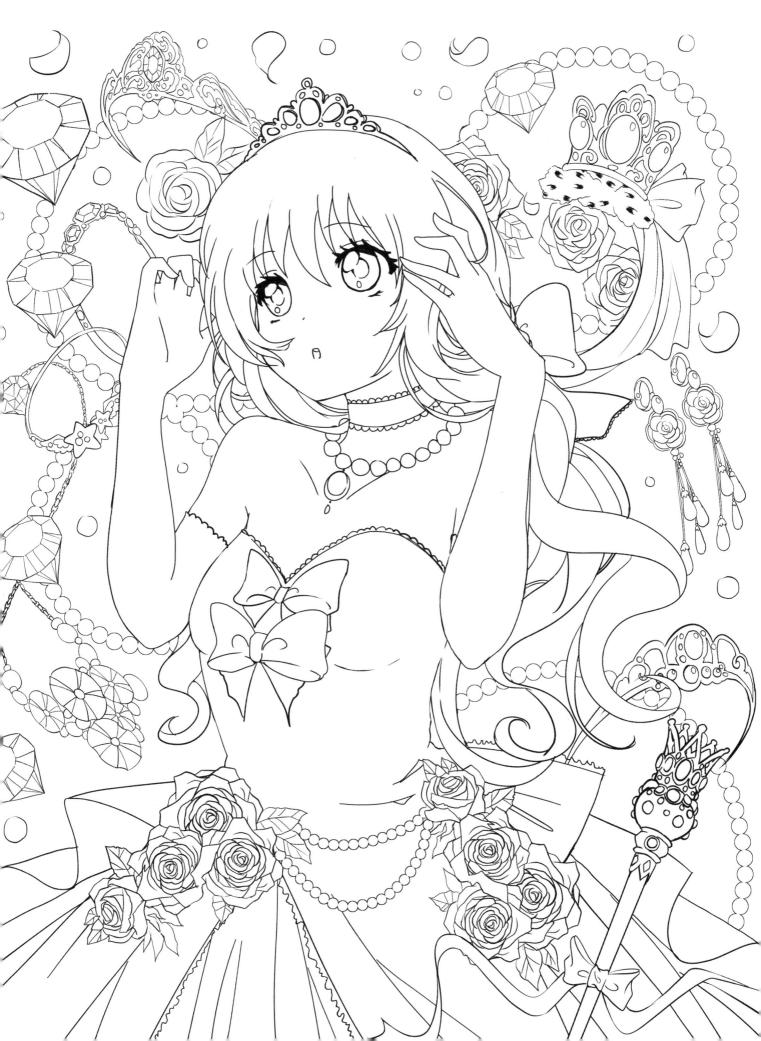

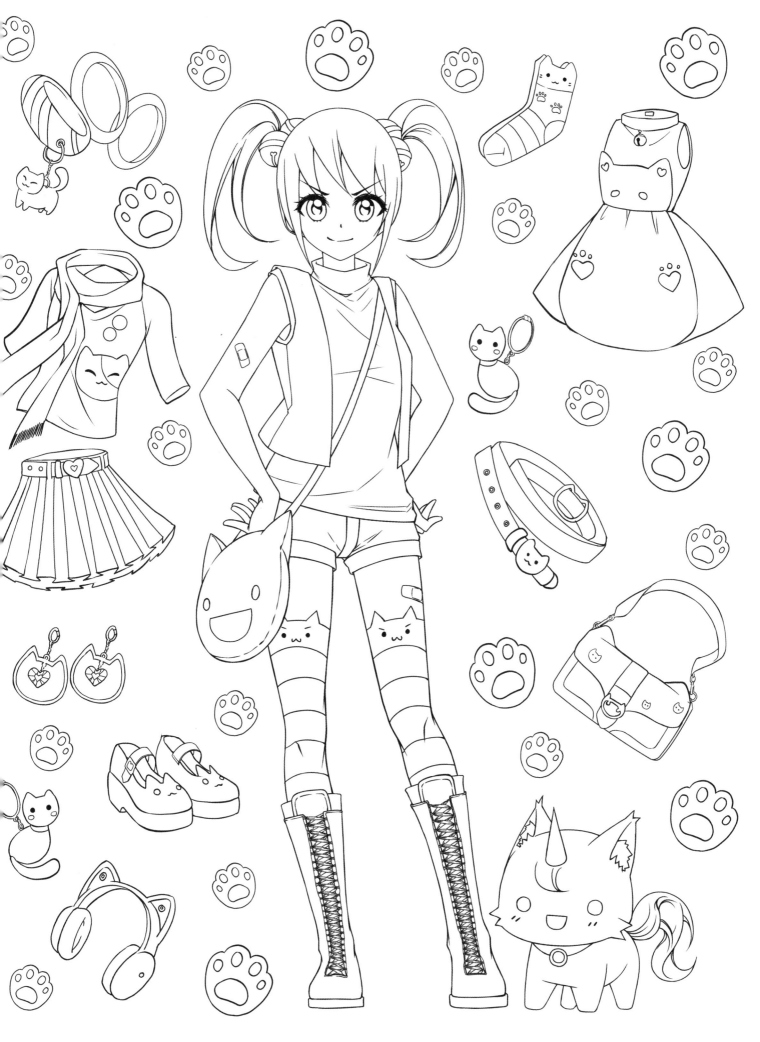

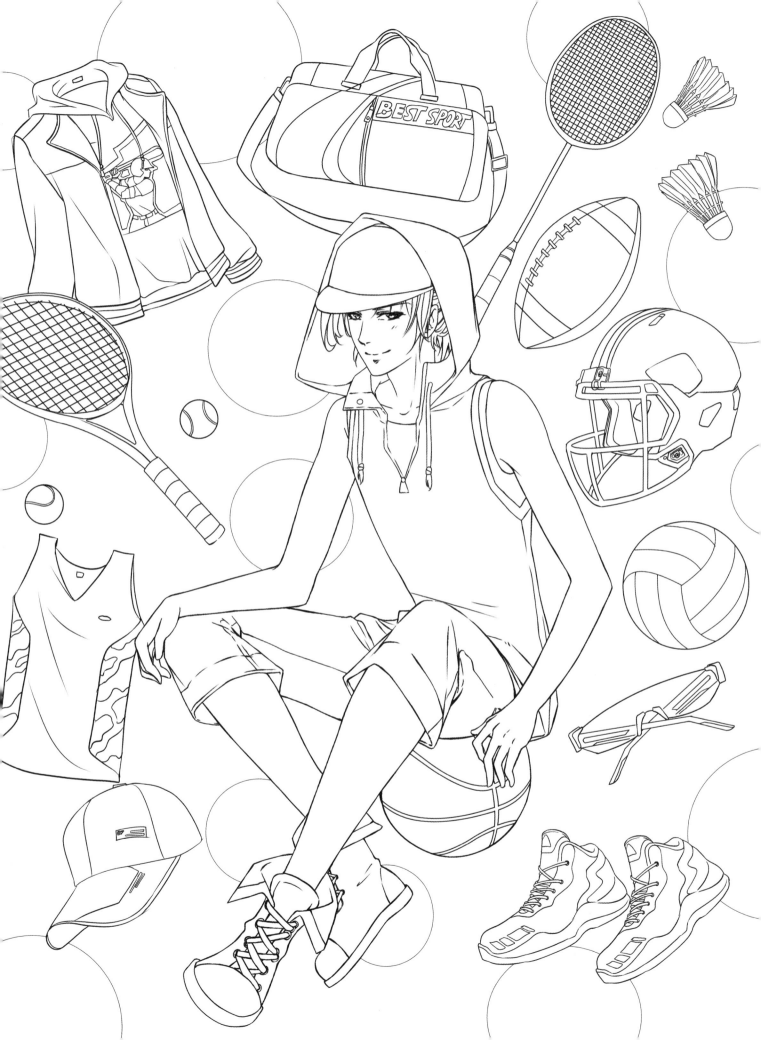

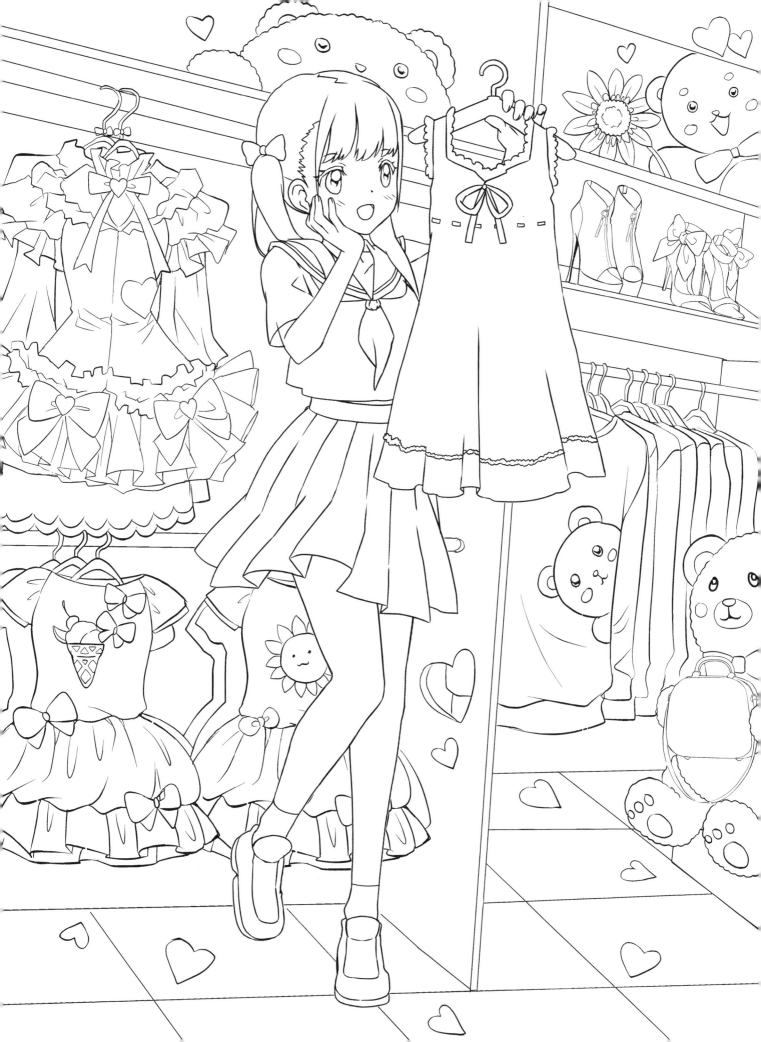

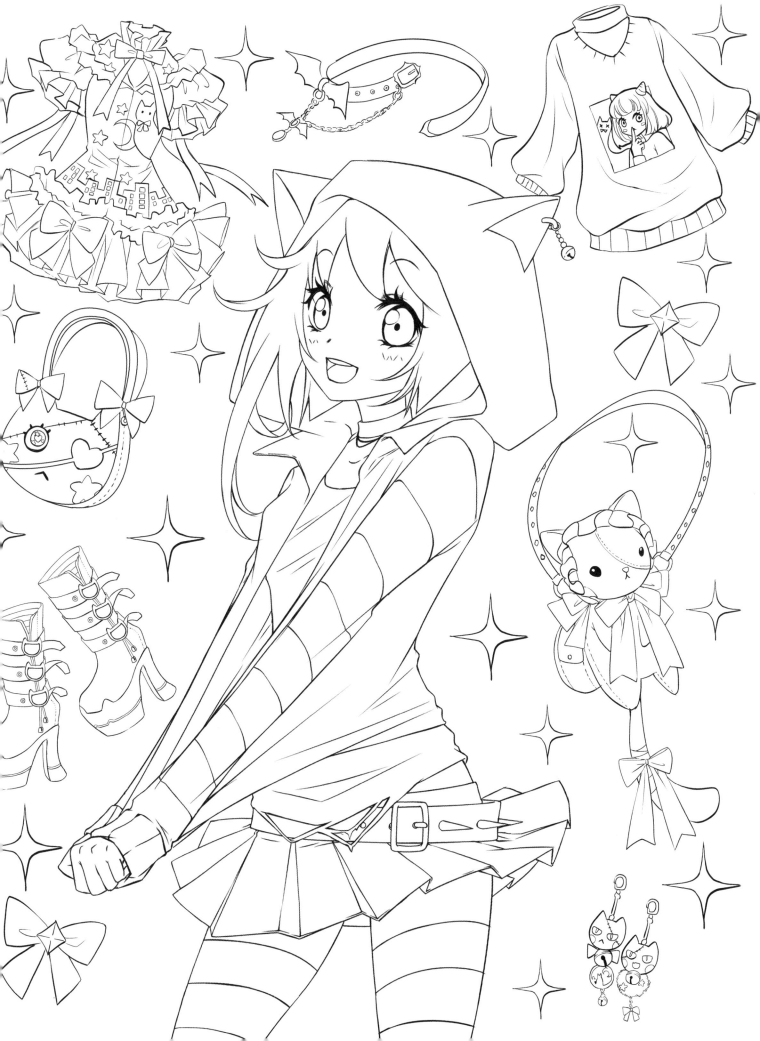

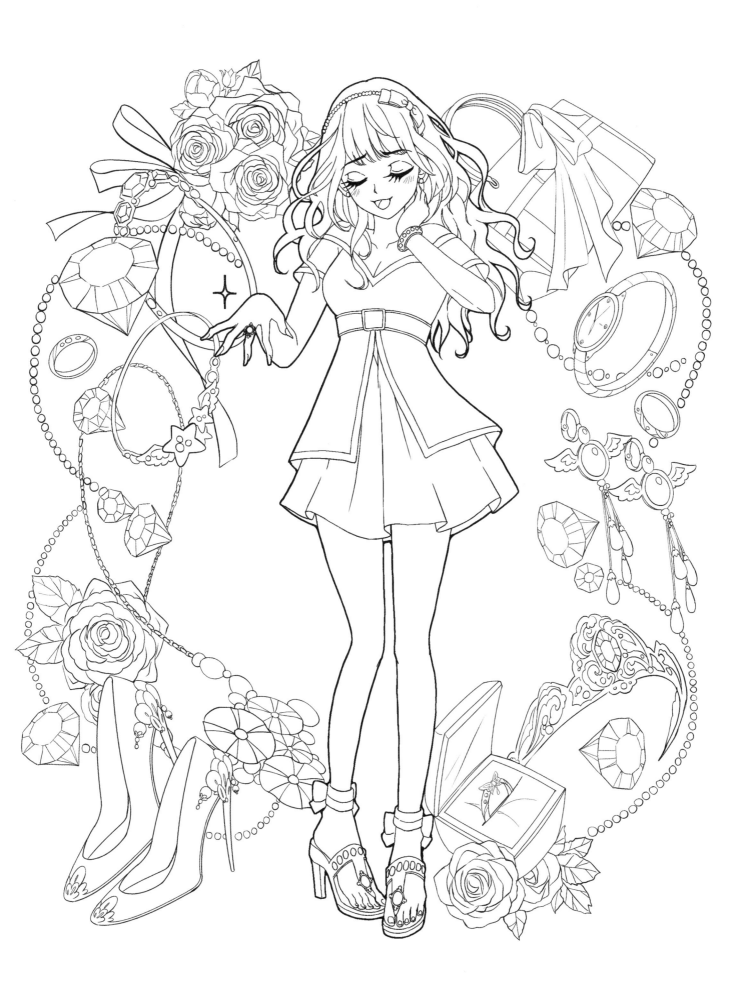

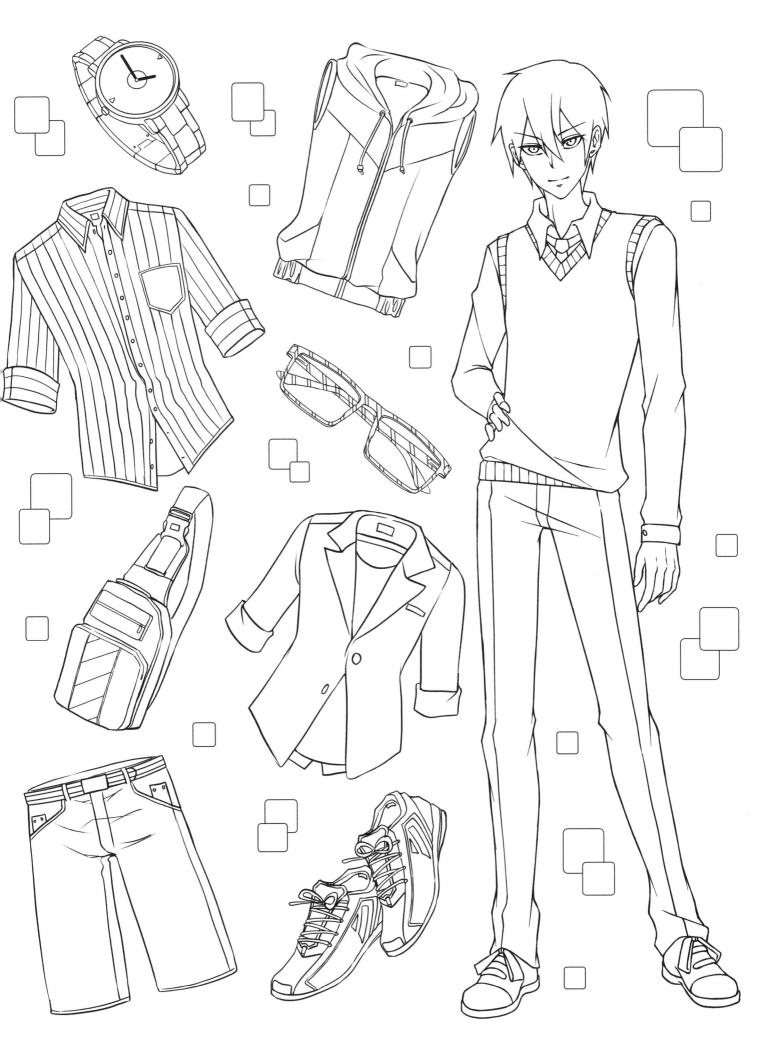

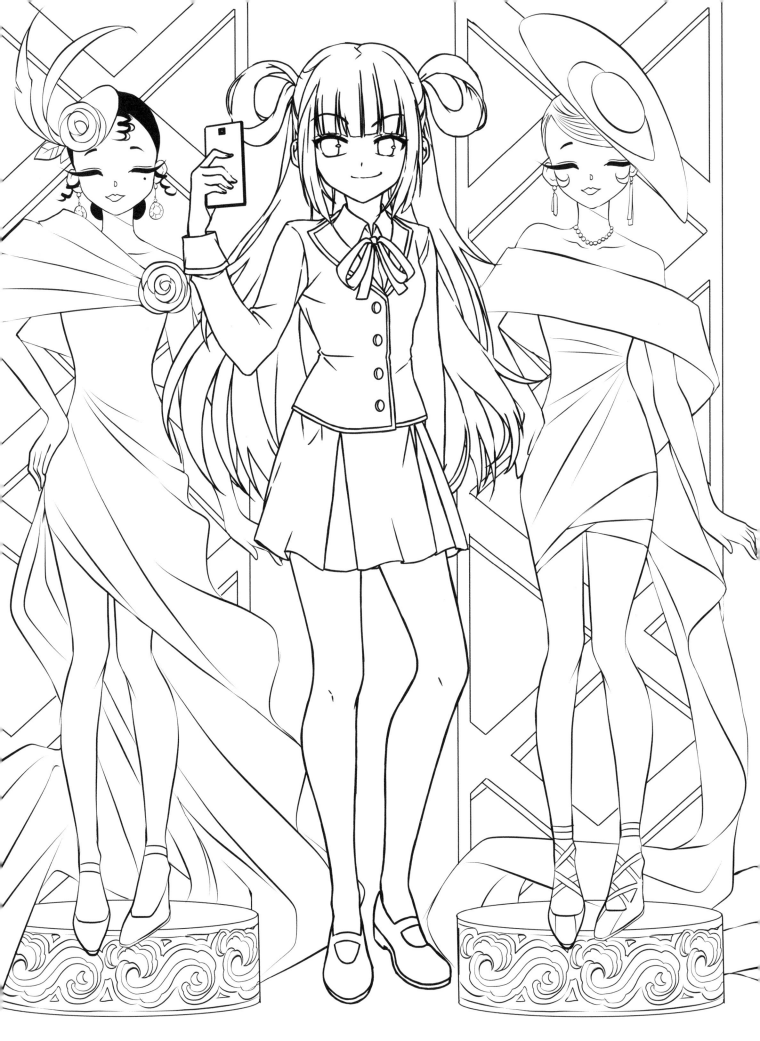

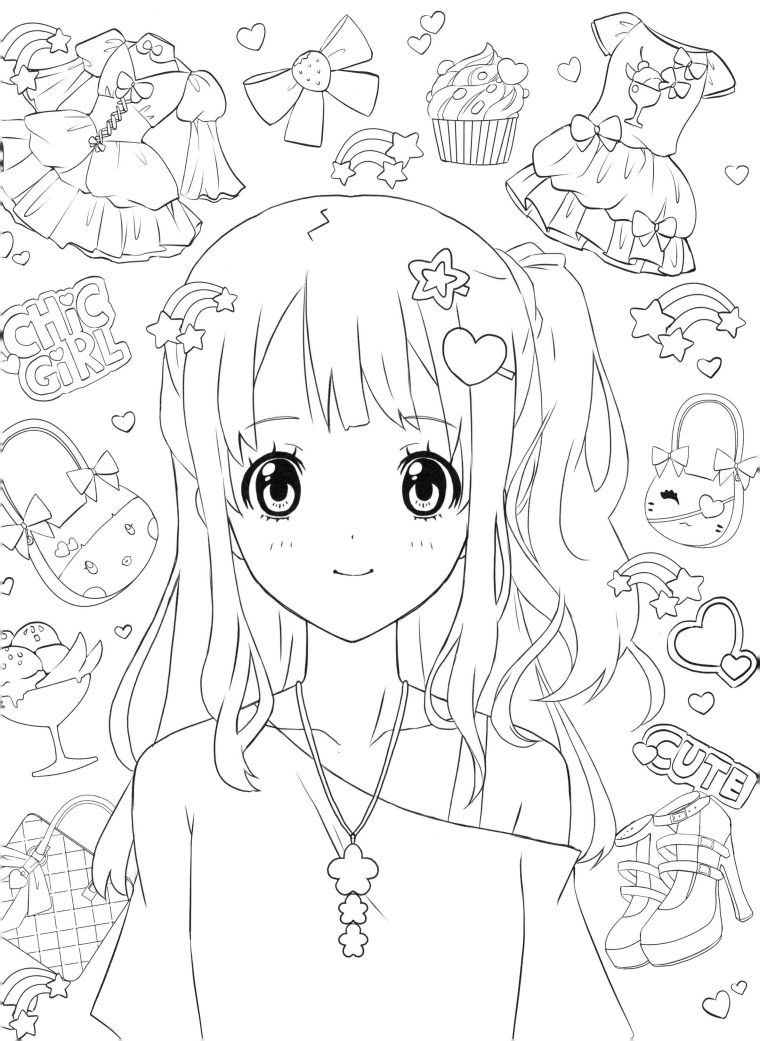

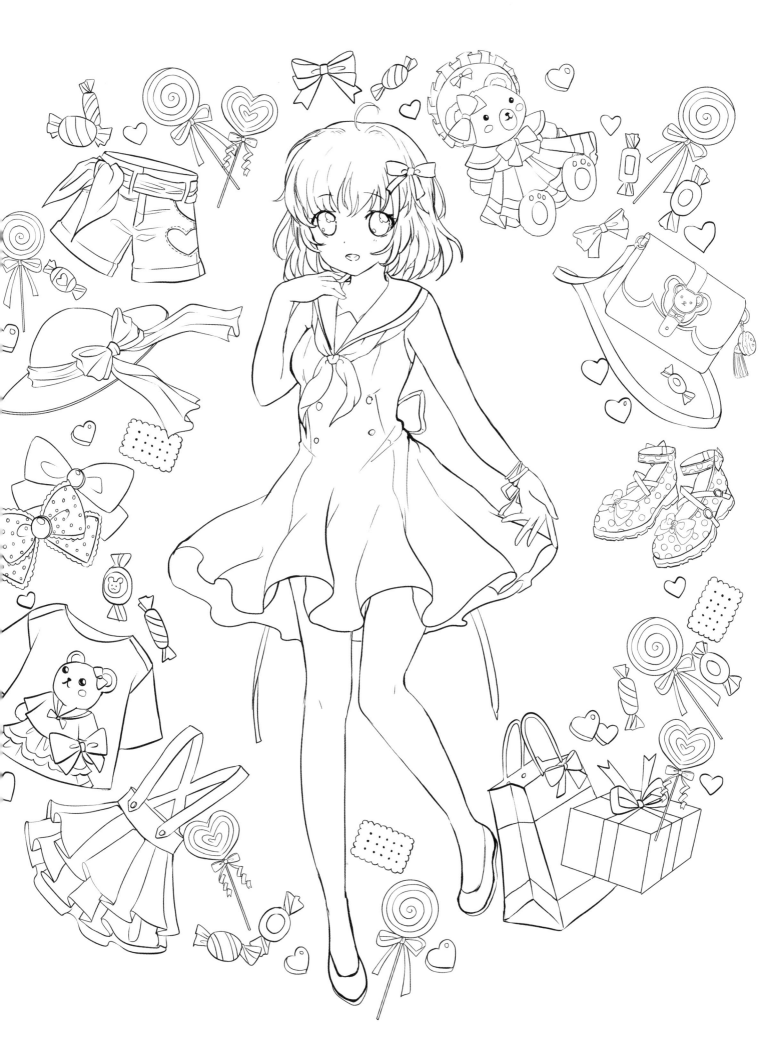

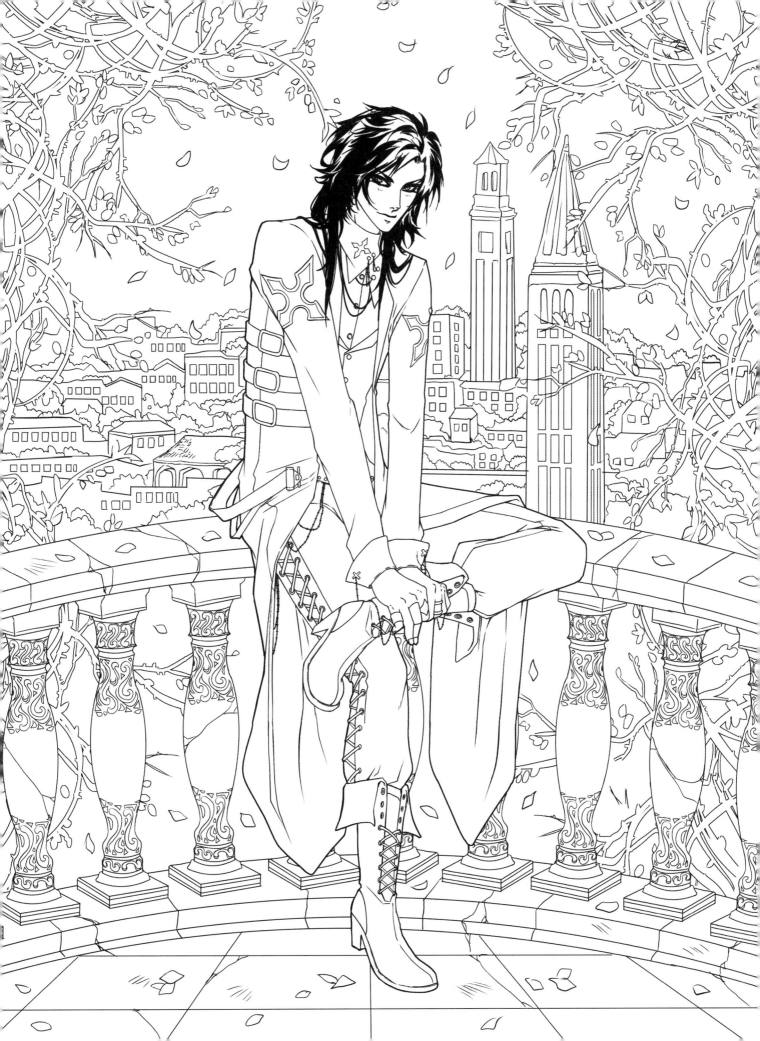

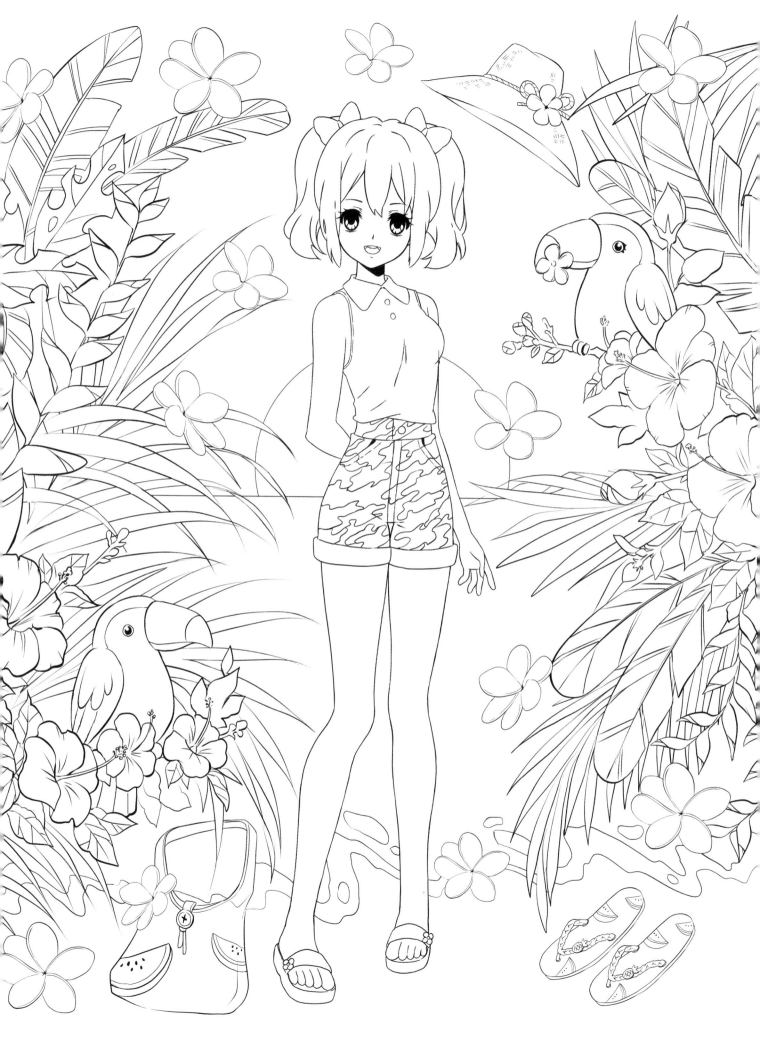

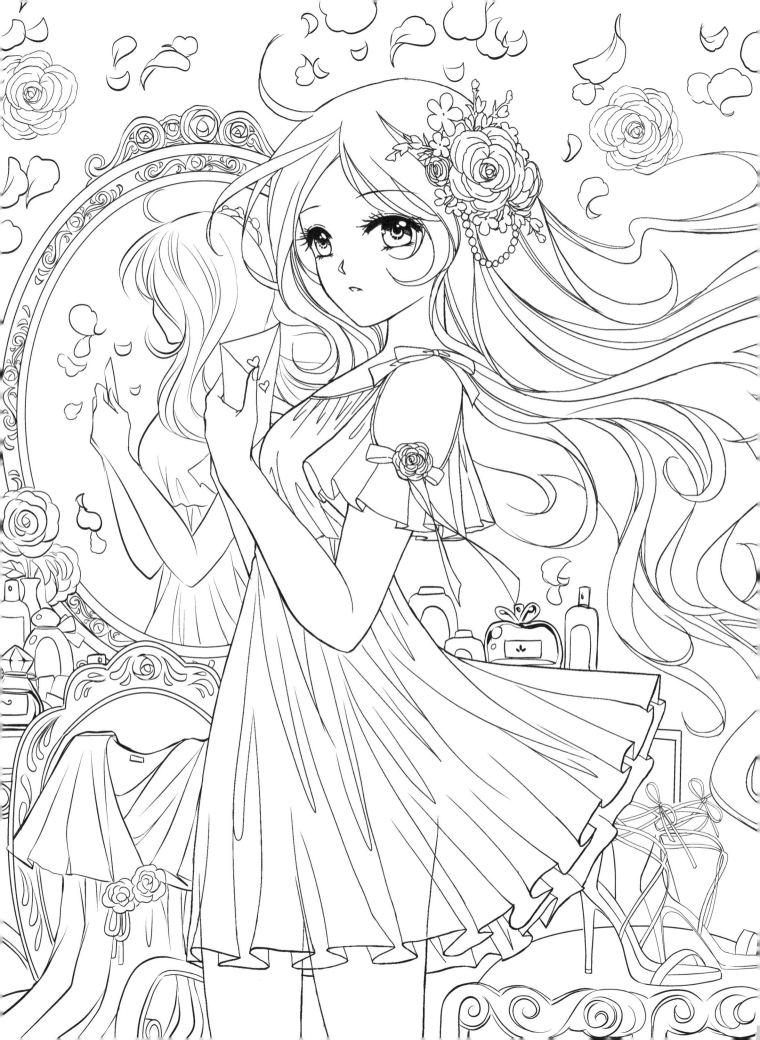

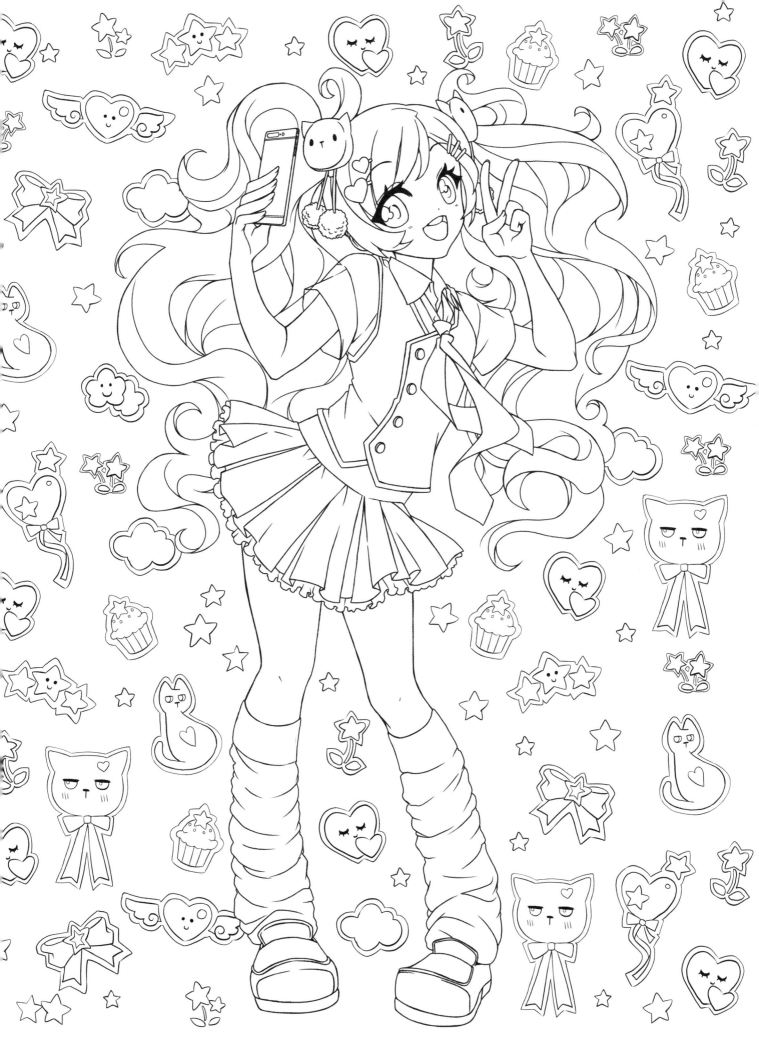

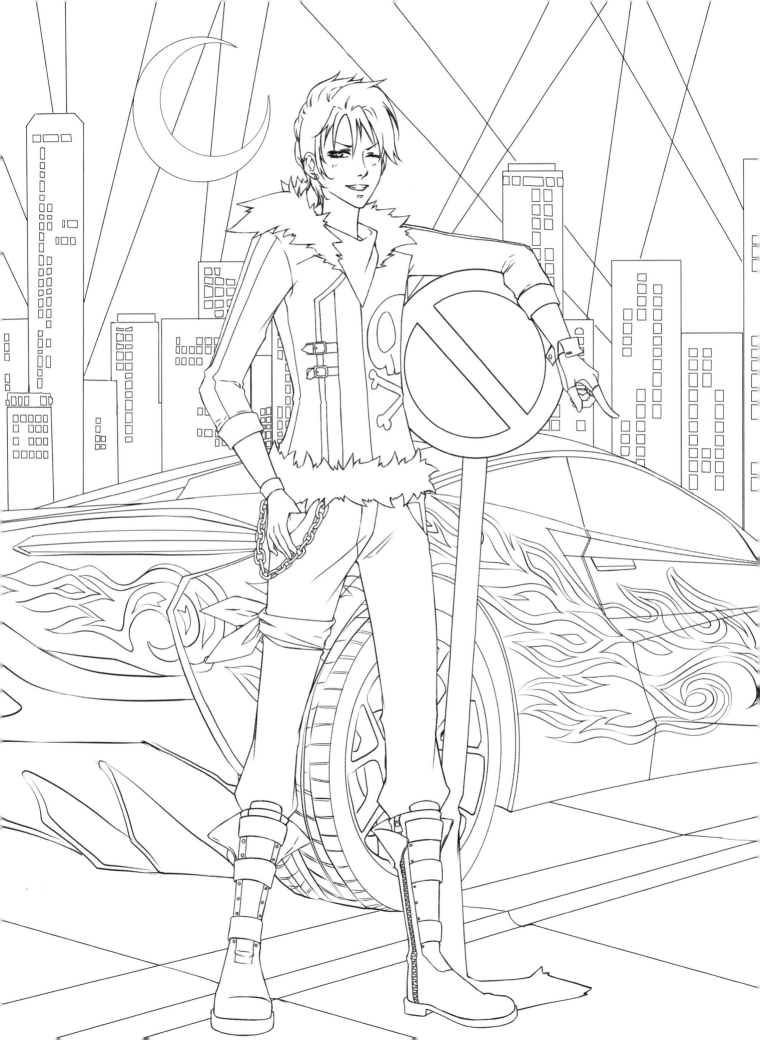

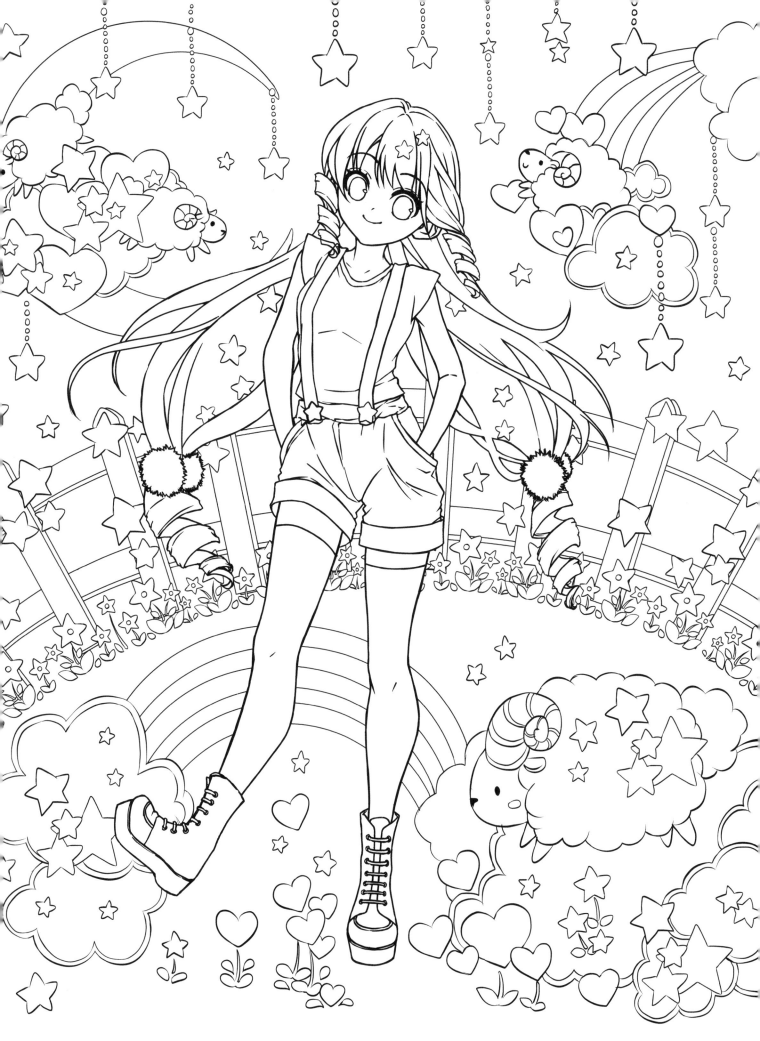

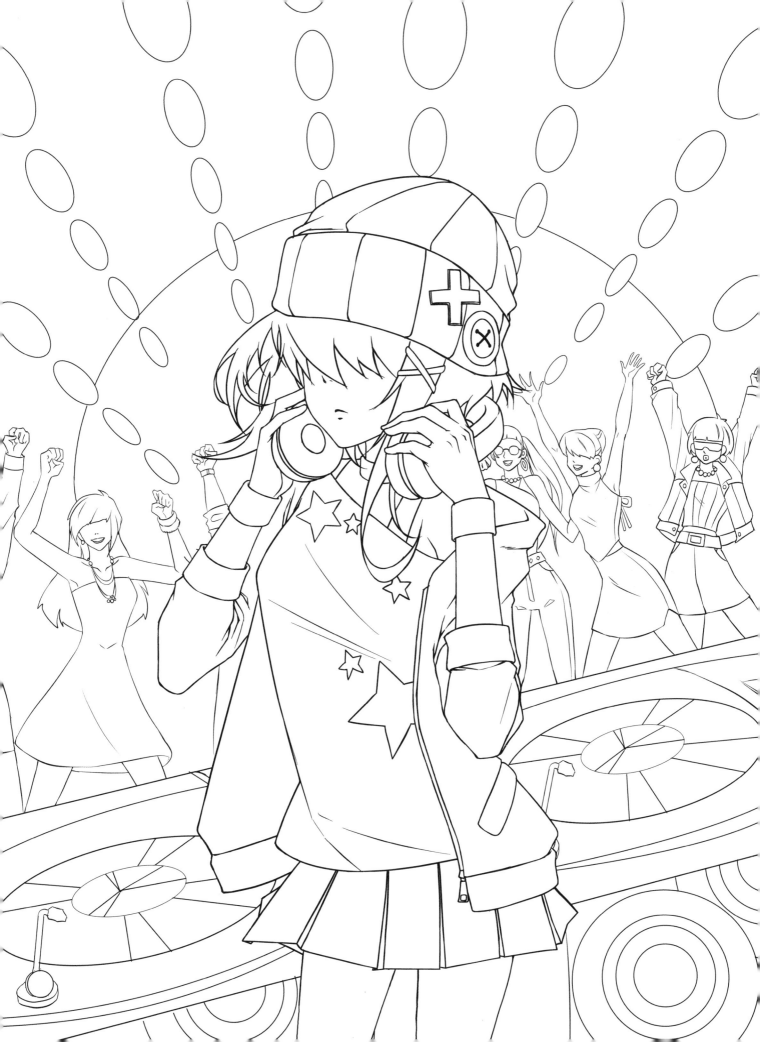

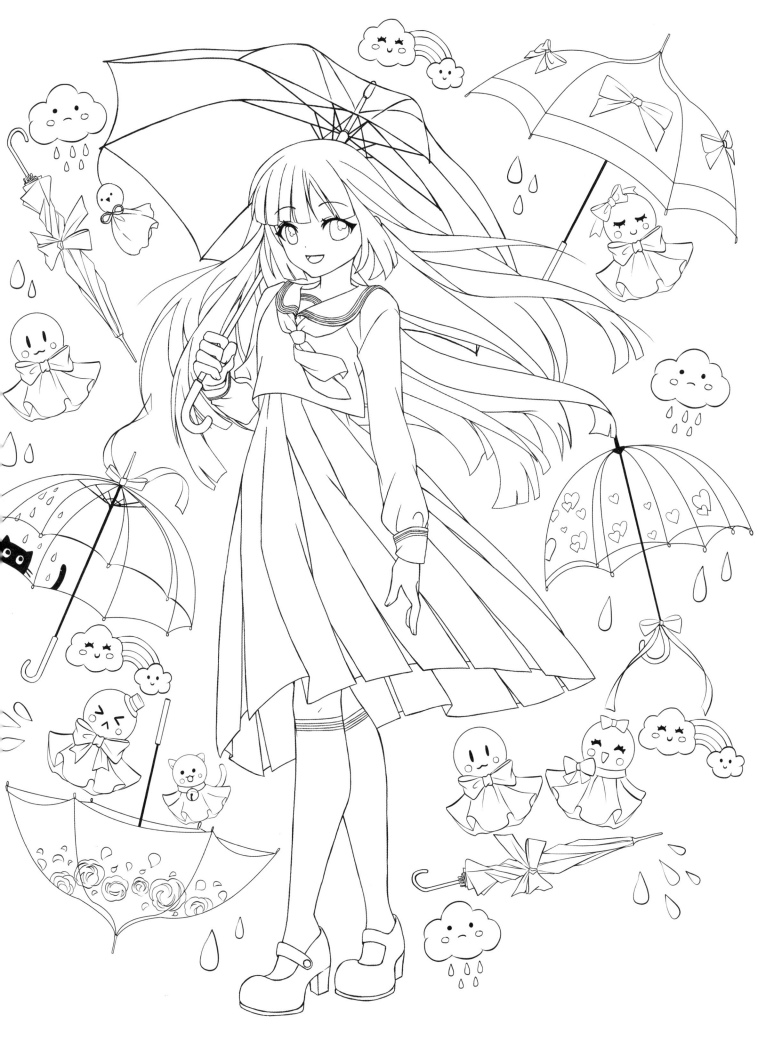

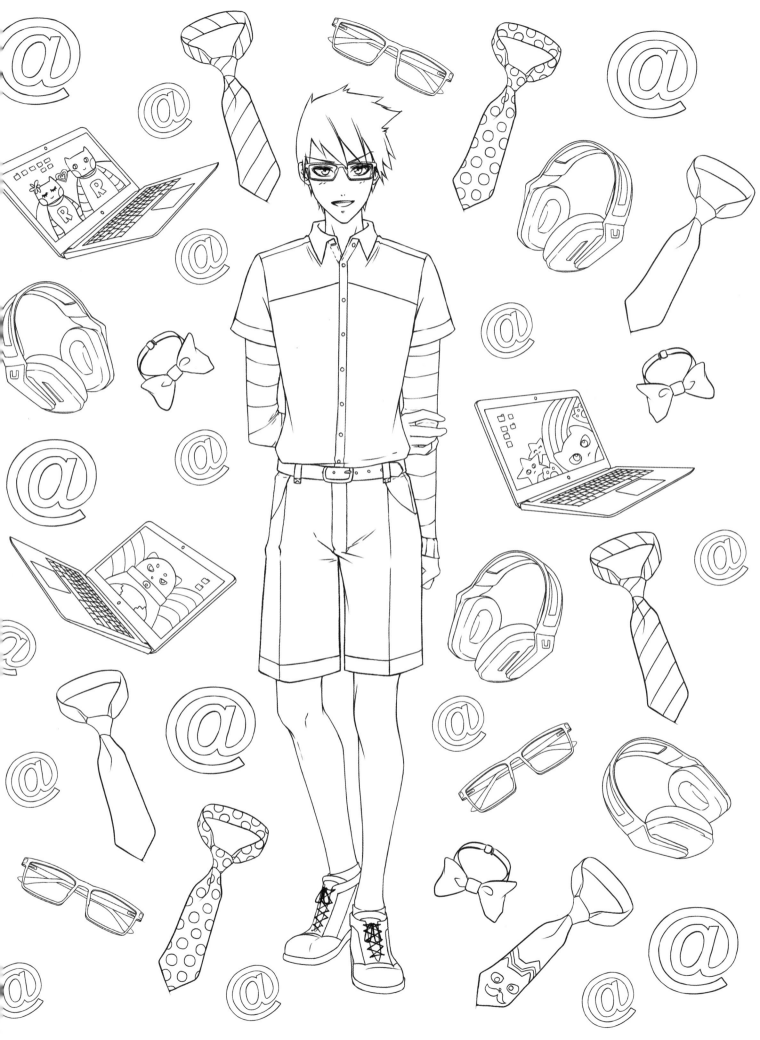

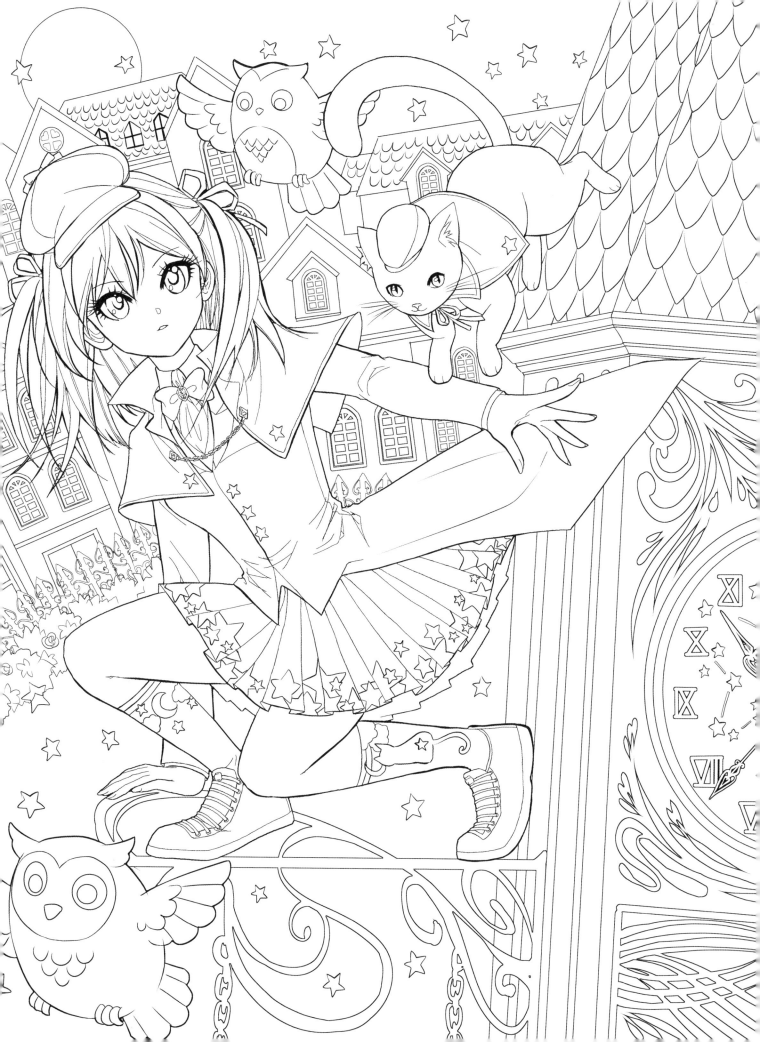

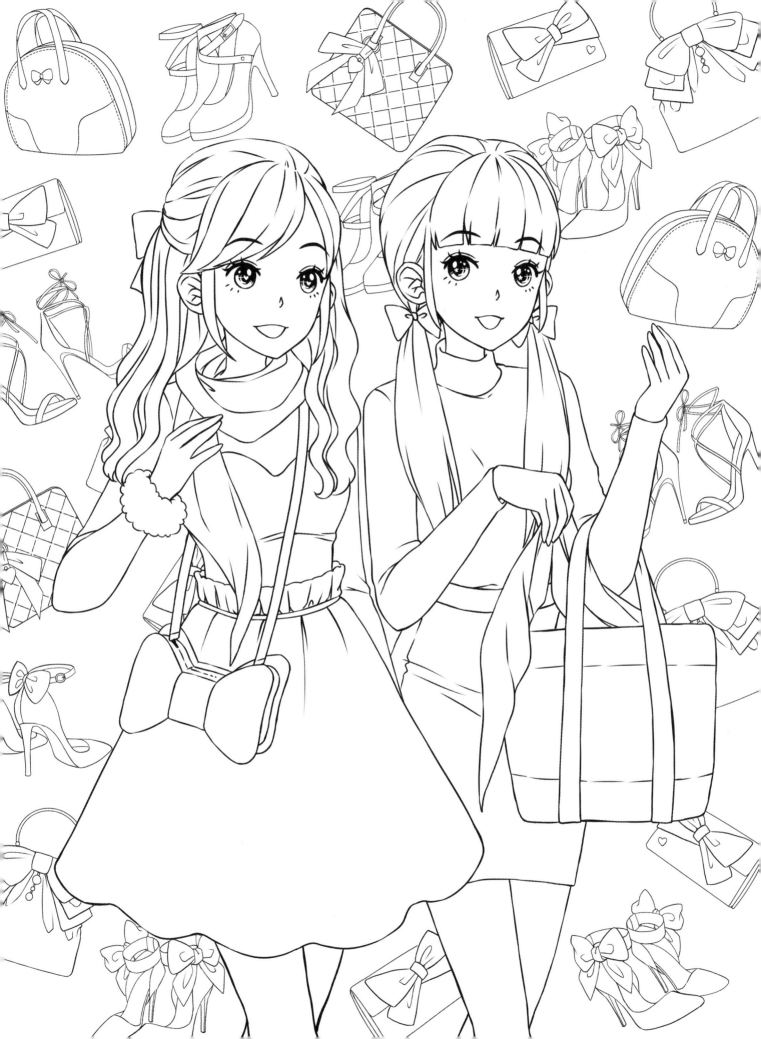

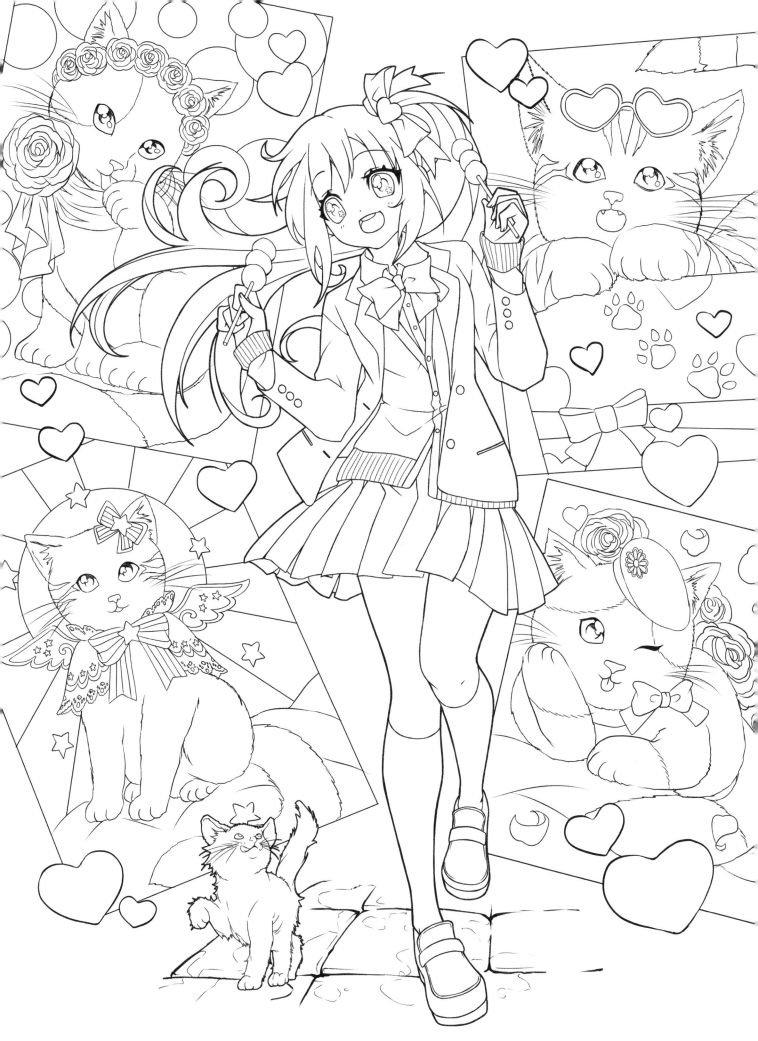

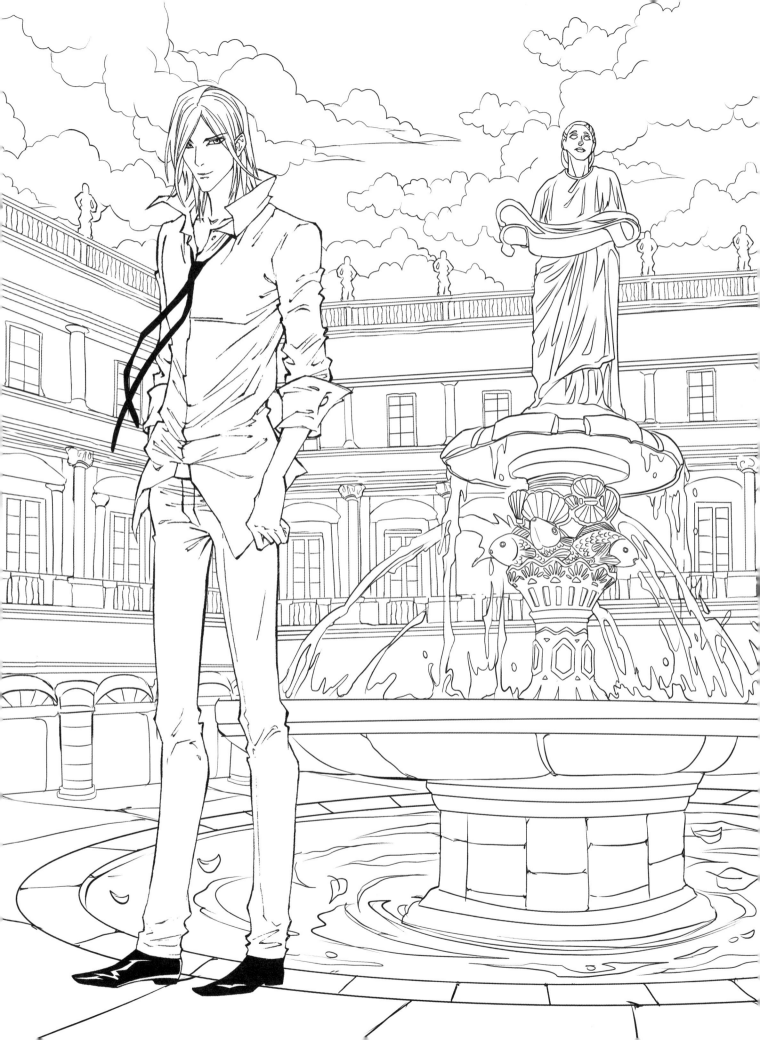

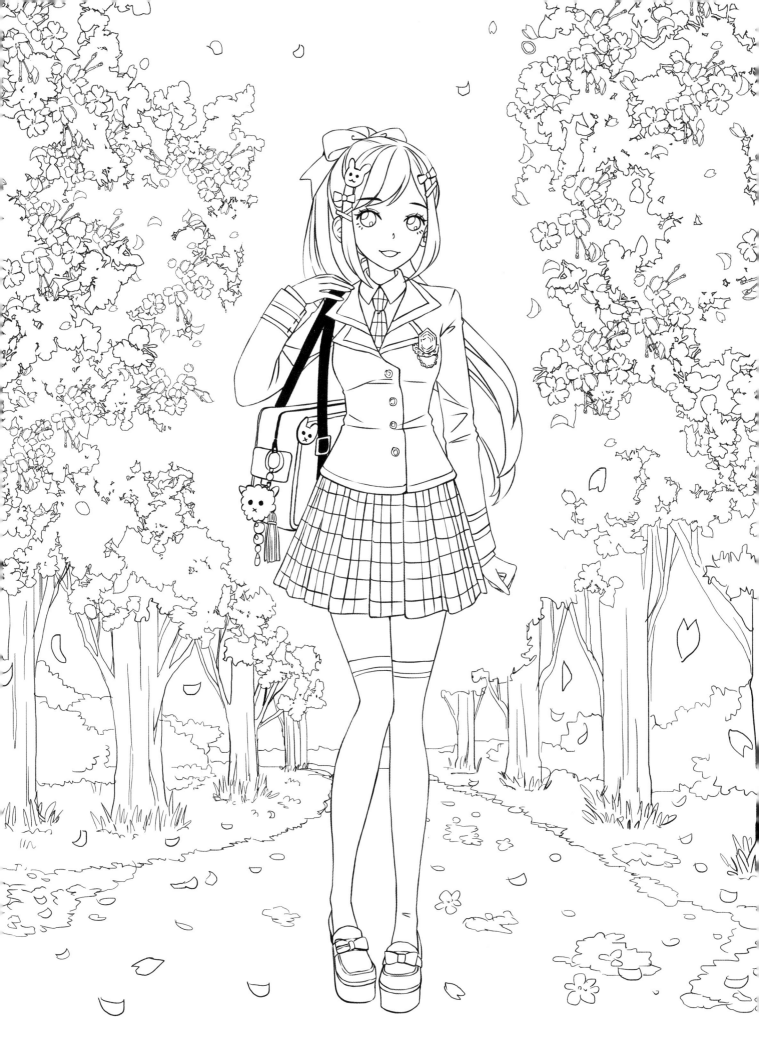

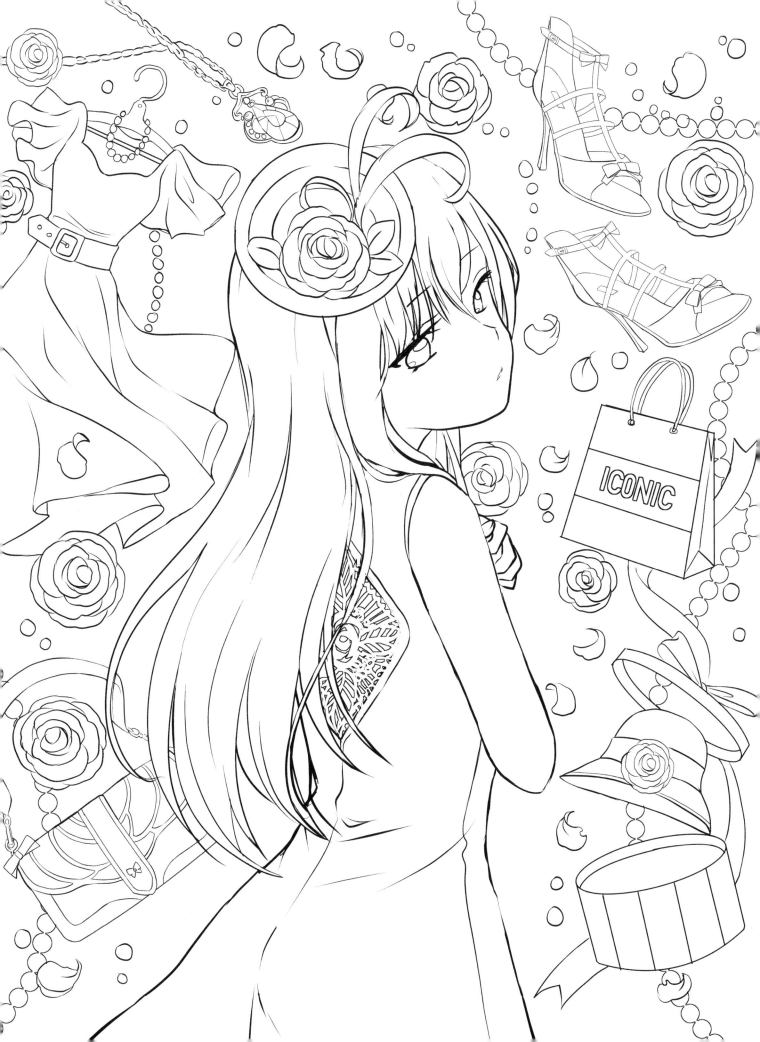

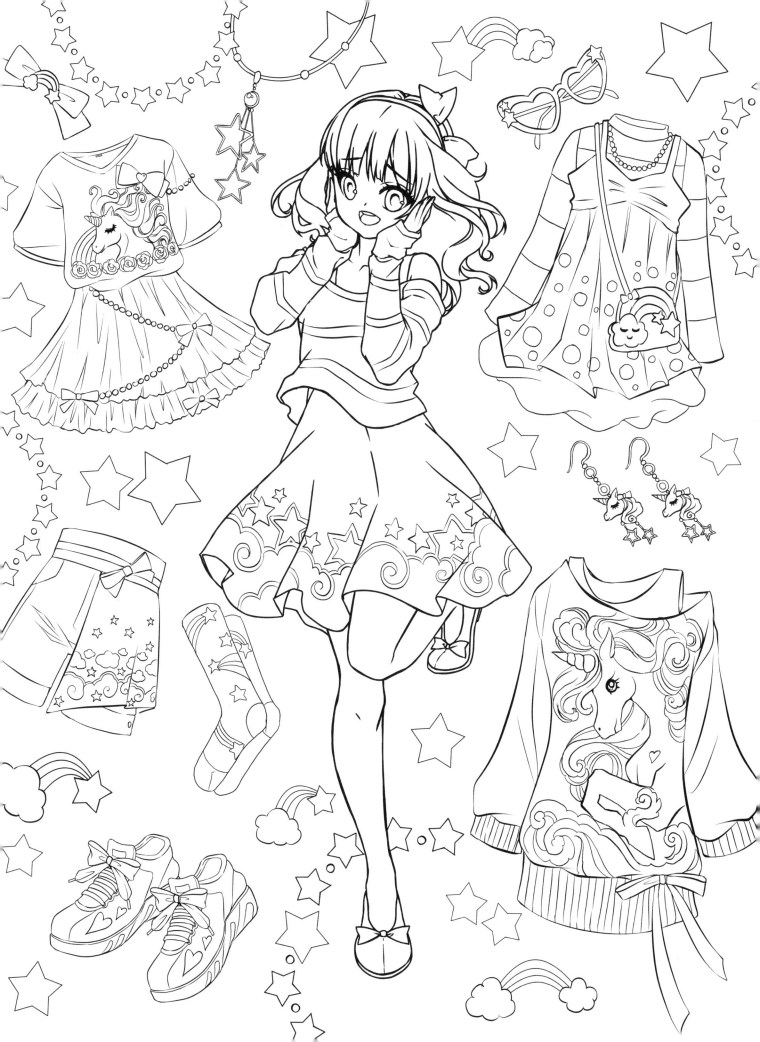

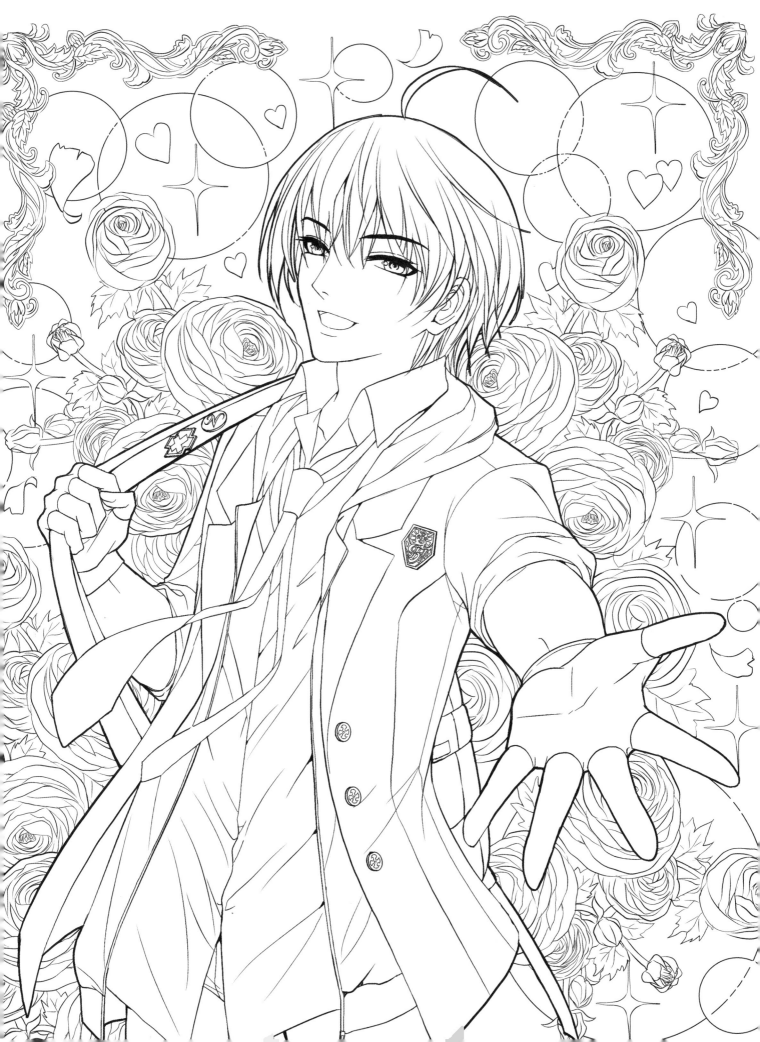

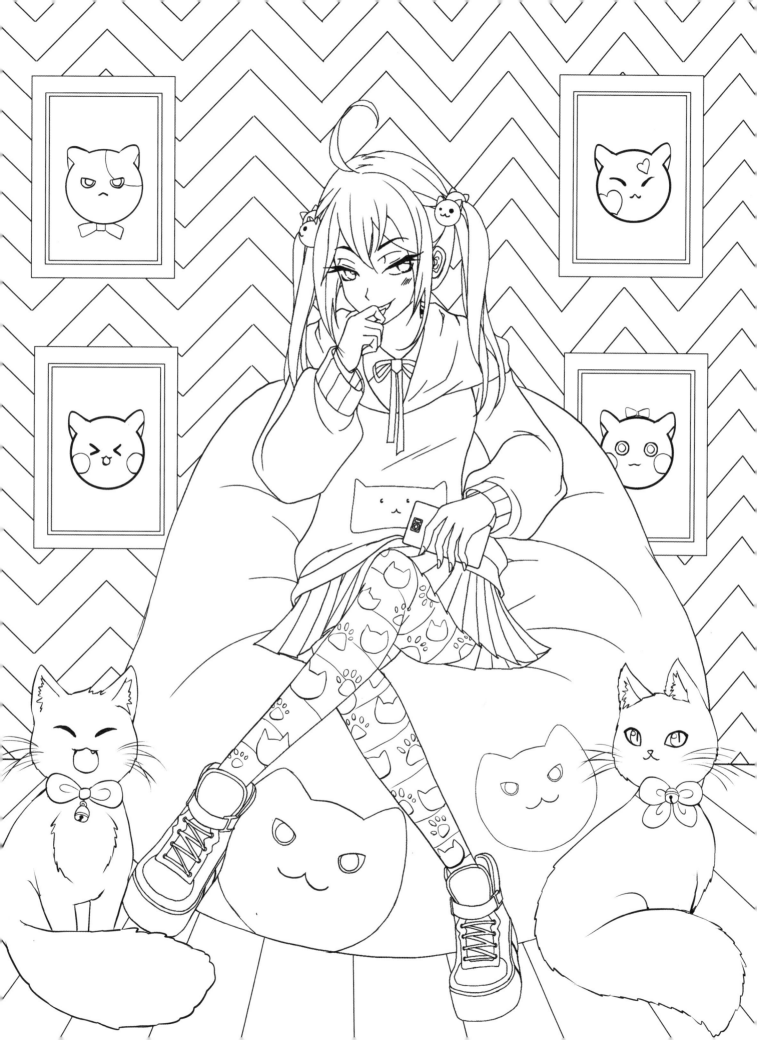

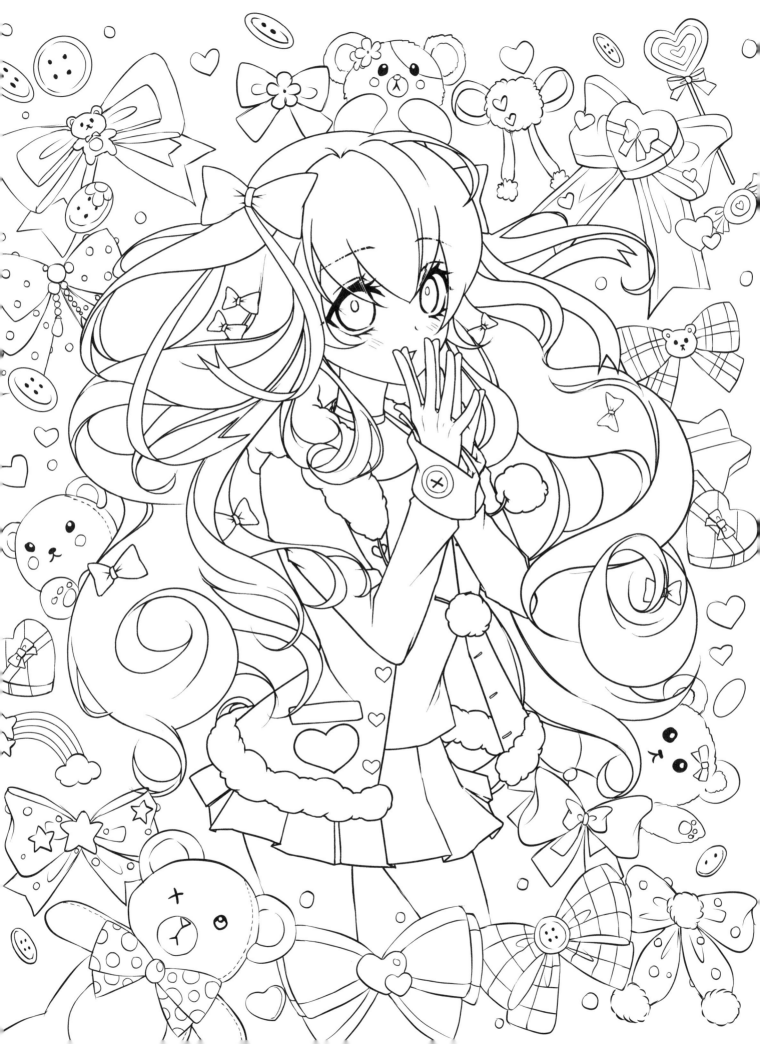

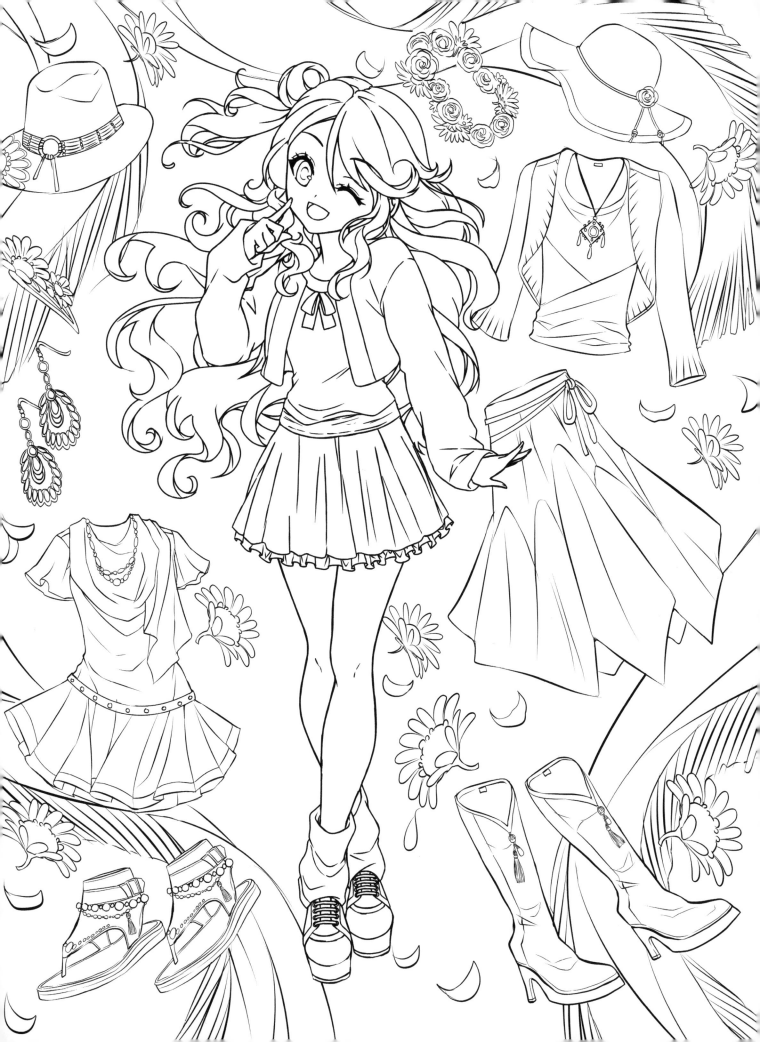

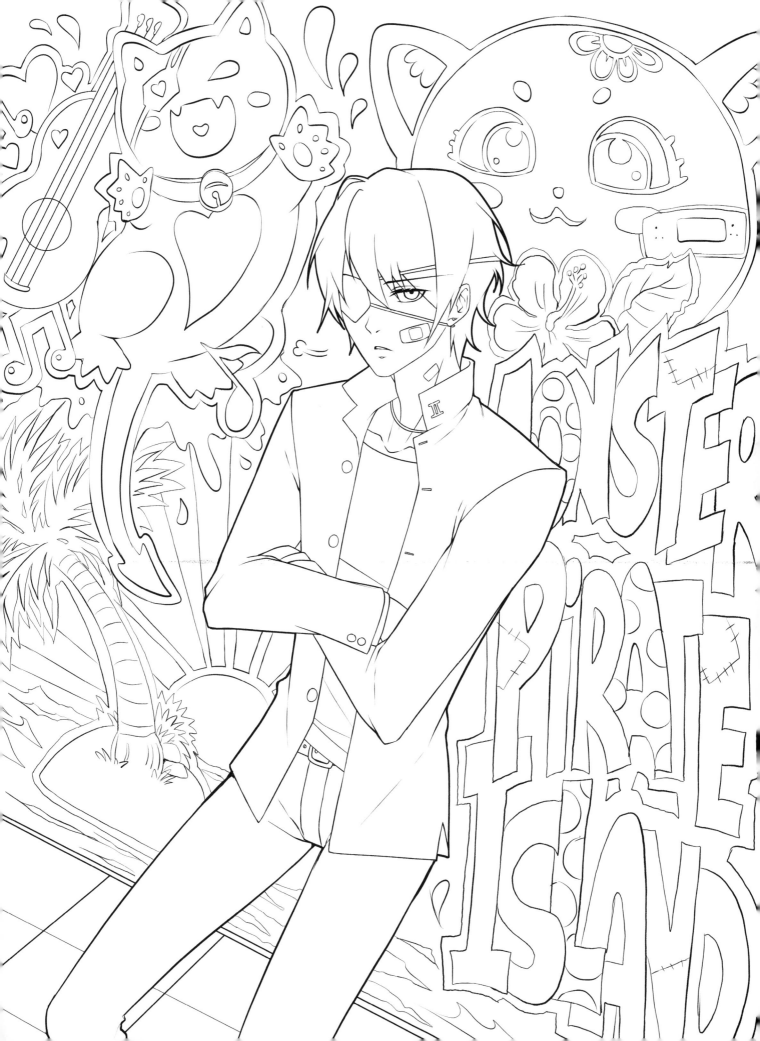

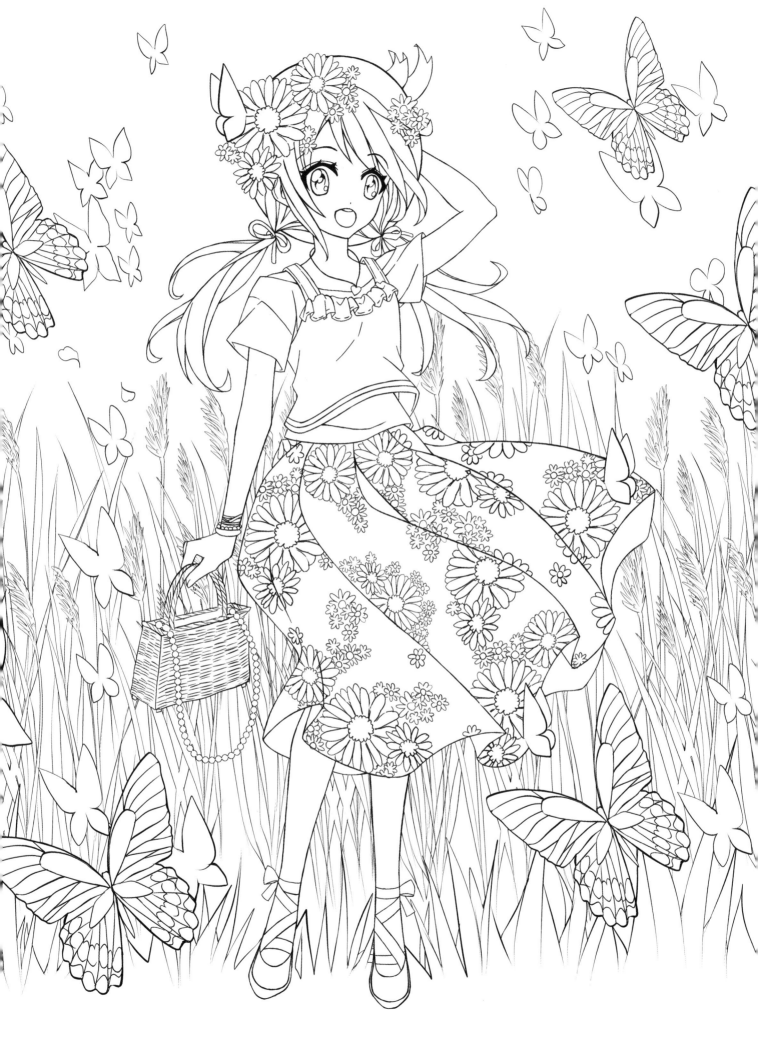

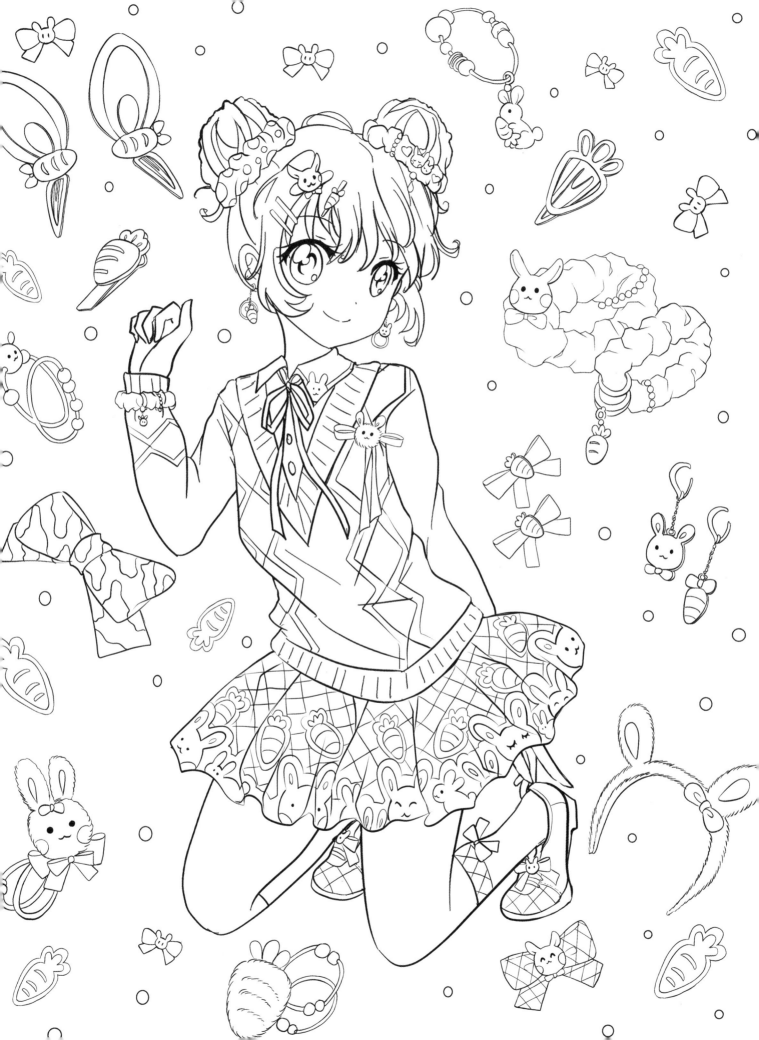

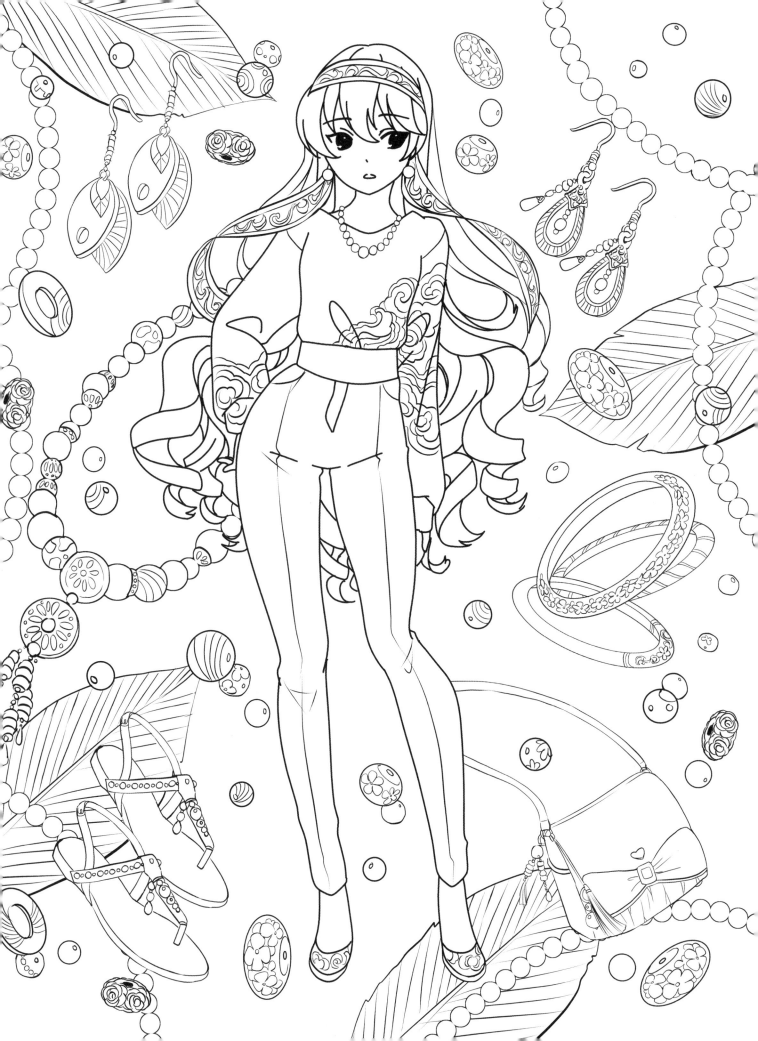

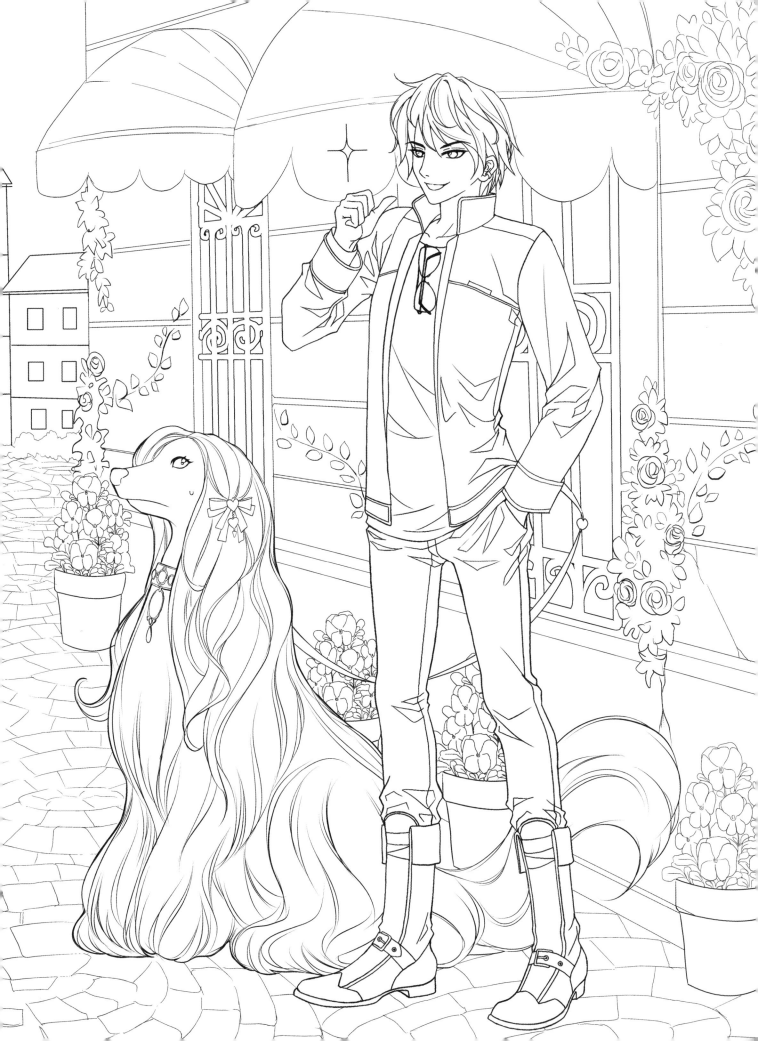

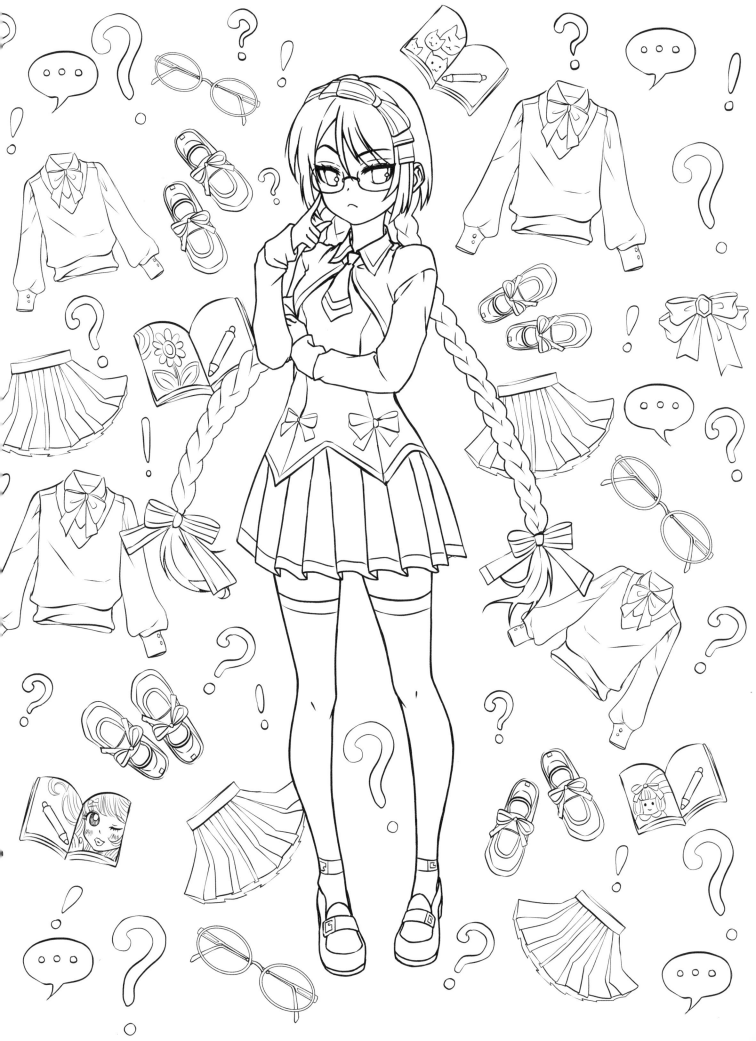

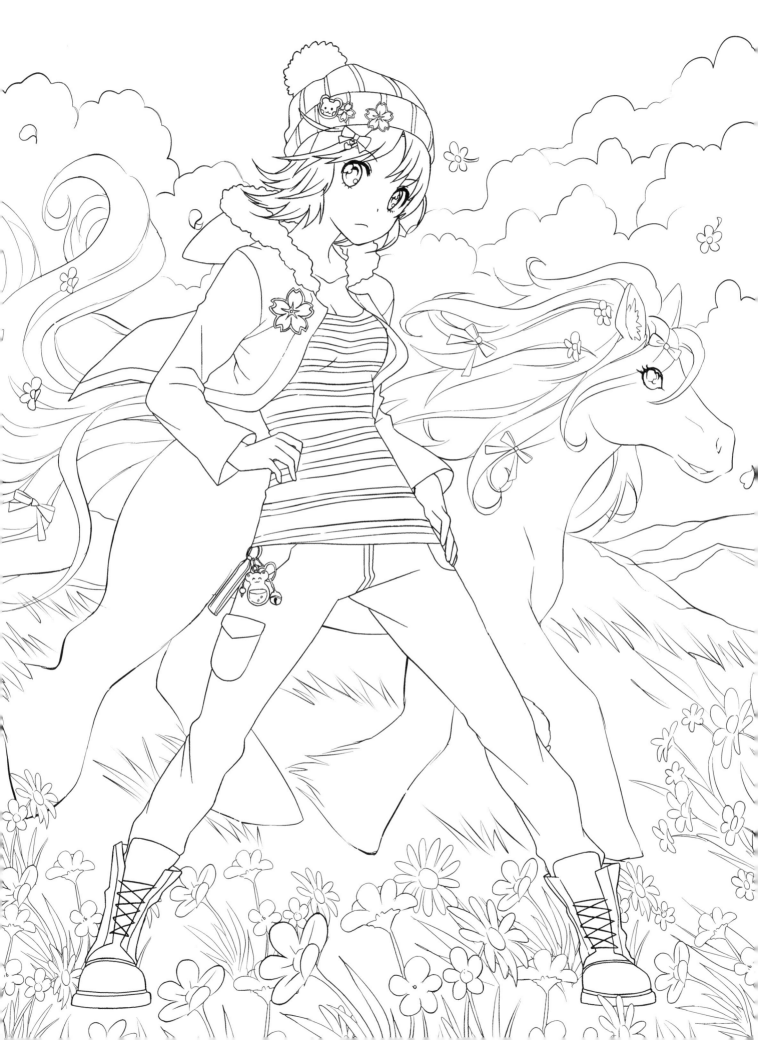

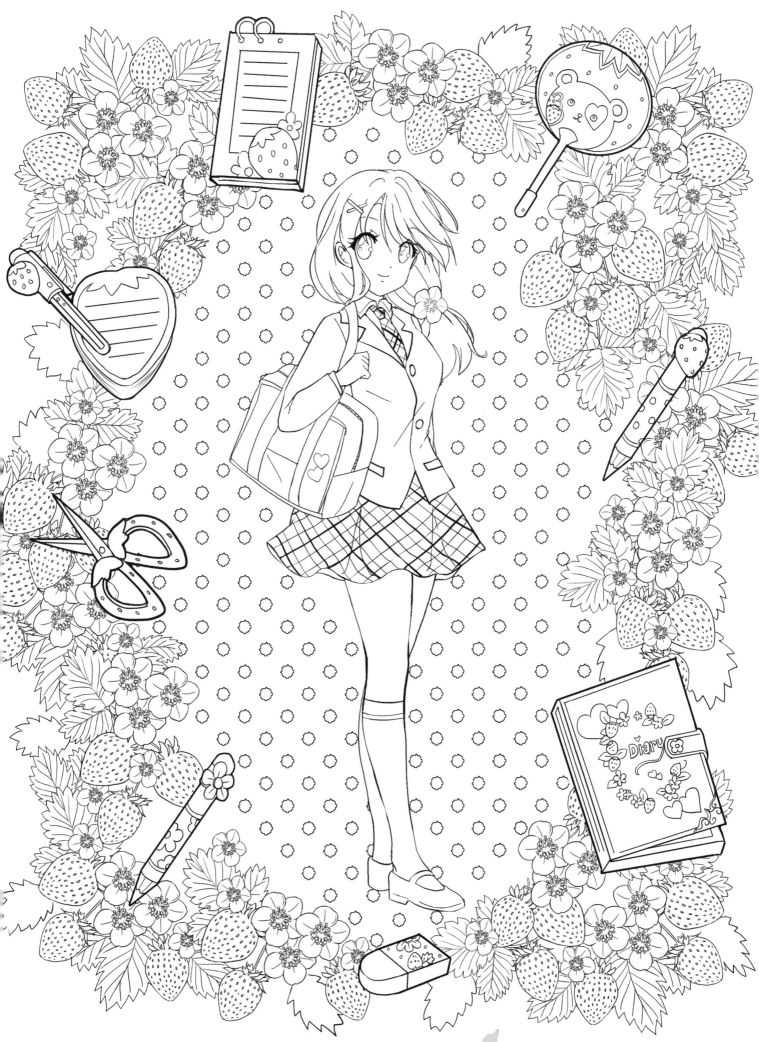

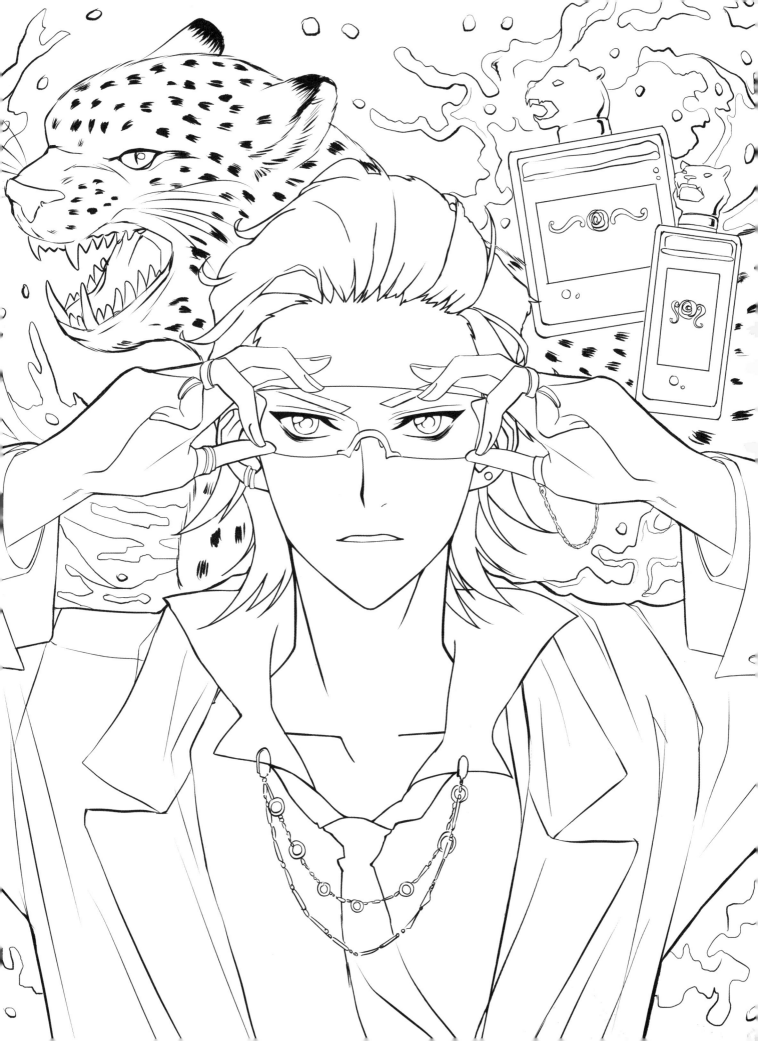

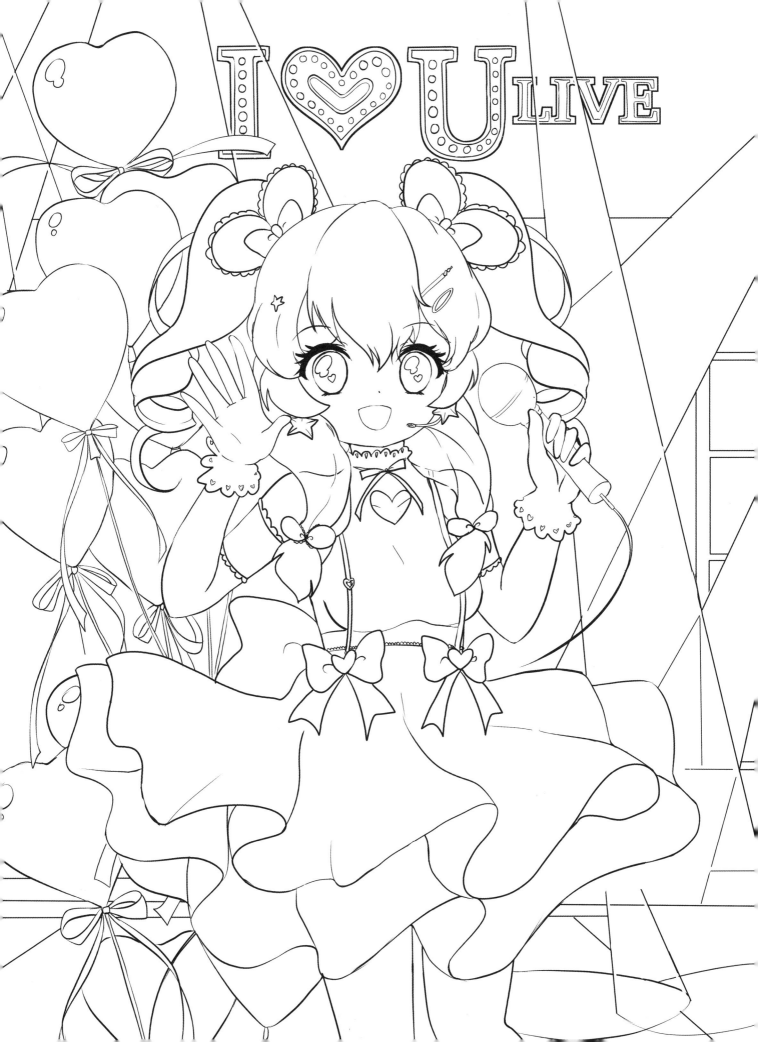

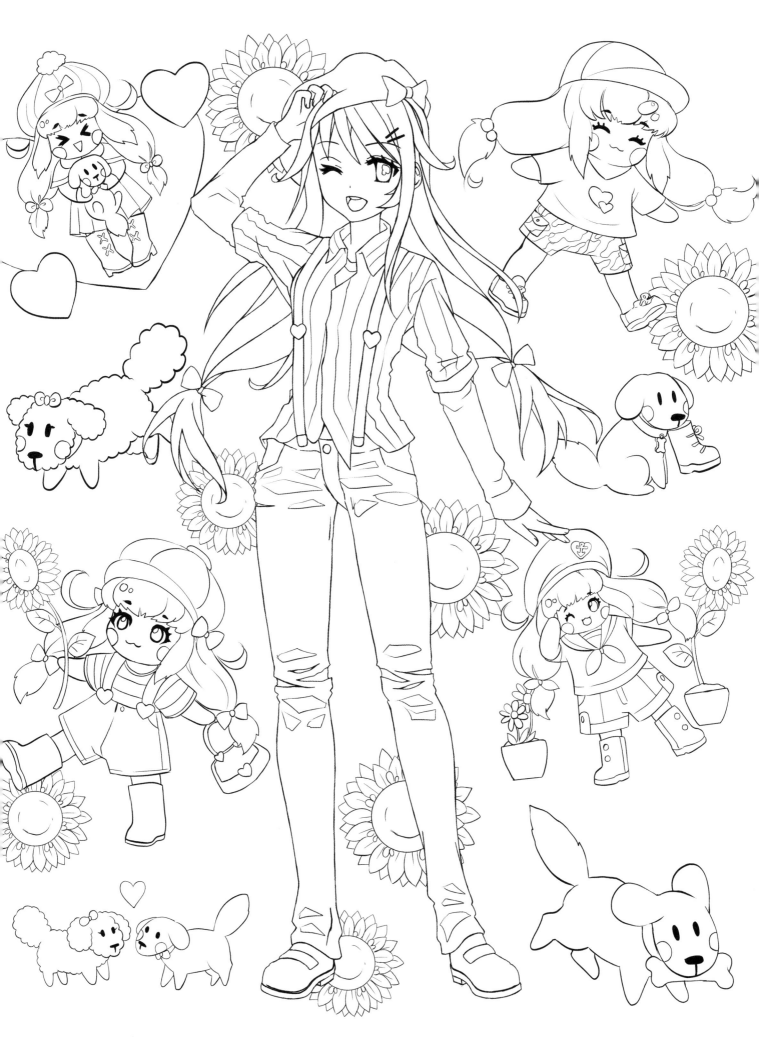

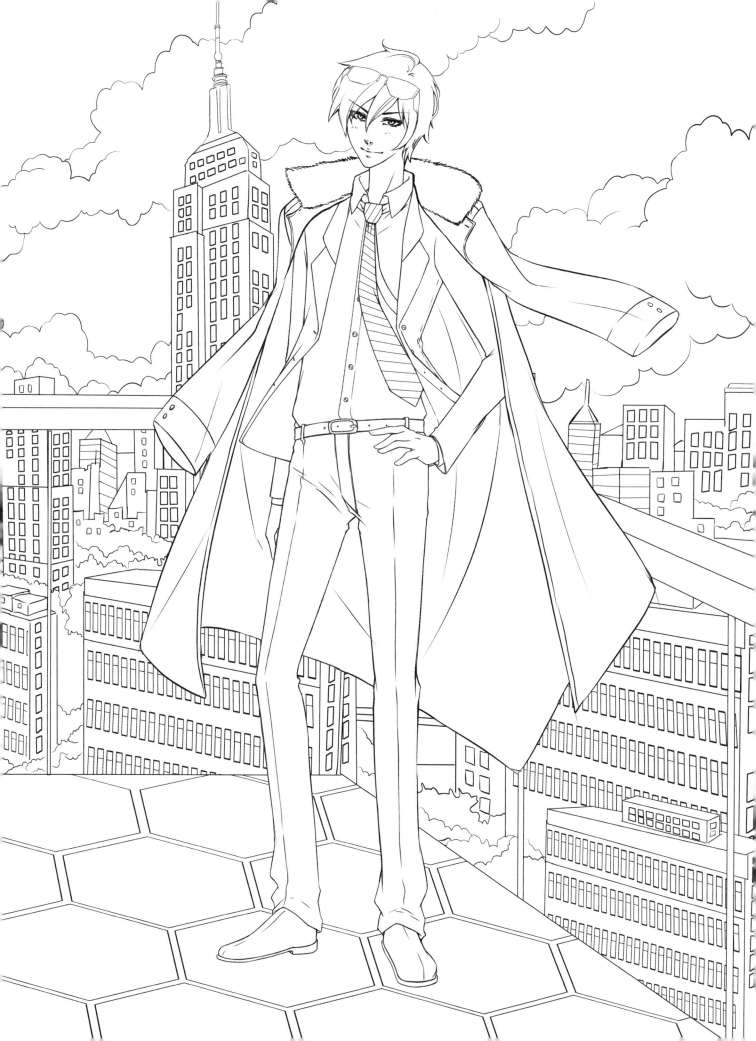